Alain Bernheim

Masonic Regularity

Westphalia Press
An imprint of Policy Studies Organization
1527 New Hampshire Ave., NW
Washington, D.C. 20036
info@ipsonet.org

ISBN-10: 1-63391-408-9
ISBN-13: 978-1-63391-408-7

Cover design by Jeffrey Barnes
jbarnesbook.design

Daniel Gutierrez-Sandoval, Executive Director
PSO and Westphalia Press

Updated material and comments on this edition
can be found at the Westphalia Press website:
www.westphaliapress.org

MASONIC REGULARITY

ALAIN BERNHEIM

Westphalia Press
An Imprint of the Policy Studies Organization
Washington, DC
2016

2015. Freemasonry's Royal Secret – The "Francken Manuscript" of the High Degrees. Introduction by Alain Bernheim, 33°, and Arturo de Hoyos, 33°, G.C. – The Scottish Rite Research Society (Washington, D.C.). ISBN 978-0-9837738-6-3

2014. Régularité Maçonnique. Paris, Éditions Télétes. ISBN 978-2-906031-97-5.

2013. Les deux plus anciens manuscrits des grades symboliques de la franc-maçonnerie de langue française. Paris, Éditions Dervy. ISBN : 979-10-242-0020-0.

2012. Ramsay et ses deux discours. Paris, Éditions Télétes. ISBN 978-2-976031-74-6.

2011. Le rite en trente-trois grades – De Frederick Dalcho à Charles Riandey. Paris, Éditions Dervy. ISBN 978-2-84454-655-5.

2008. Une certaine idée de la franc-maçonnerie. Paris, Éditions Dervy. ISBN 978-2-84454-564-0.

— Introduction and index to the reprint of *Outline on the Rise and Progress of Freemasonry in Louisiana* by James B. Scot. Afterword by Michael R. Poll. Second Cornerstone Edition. New Orleans, Louisiana, USA. ISBN 1-934935-31-X. ISBN 13: 978-1-934935-31-6.

2004. [Co-author of] Freemasonry in Context - History, Ritual, Controversy. Edited by Arturo de Hoyos and S. Brent Morris. Lexington Books. USA. ISBN 0-7391-0781-X.

1994. Les Débuts de la Franc-Maçonnerie à Genève et en Suisse - Avec un Essai de Répertoire et de Généalogie des Loges de Genève (1736-1994). Genève-Paris: Champion-Slatkine. ISBN 2-05-101316-0.

And some 150 papers in *Heredom, Ars Quatuor Coronatorum, the Square, Renaissance Traditionnelle, Villard de Honnecourt, Points de vue initiatiques, Alpina, Eleusis* etc.

http://alainbernheim.wix.com/alain-bernheim

TABLE OF CONTENTS

APPENDICES

This study is intended for those who do not believe they hold the truth but are seeking it, which is more Masonic and praiseworthy. This study will not provide this truth, but arguments for them to meditate and weigh.

J. Corneloup
"Plaidoyer pour le Grand Architecte de l'Univers,"
Le Symbolisme 245 (December 1945).

But why would the United Grand Lodge of England alone have the right to "decree regularity"? And suppose, by some misfortune—and may the Grand Architect not allow it—it were to become "irregular," how would we know?

René Guilly
Renaissance Traditionnelle 17–18 (1974): 57.

You are an Apprentice, a Fellow-Craft, or a young Master. Perhaps even a Grand Master or a Grand Commander. You have read much. You are lucky, if you are a French Freemason, to live in 2014 because 2014 is an essential year for French Freemasonry. Just over two centuries ago, it was united. This union lasted no more than five years.

Today, it is again seeking to unite. It is not a simple undertaking, because over two centuries many habits have been built up.

Since this union is on its way, some Freemasons, sometimes qualified as authorized or regarded with a grain of notoriety, have made considerable efforts to sabotage this union with "indisputable" claims that were inaccurate, fanciful, or originated in their sole imagination. I quoted a few under *Anthologies*. For instance:

Anthology I

It is however indisputable that, without recognition from London, a Grand Lodge is not regular.

Roger DACHEZ, 2011[1]

This type of untruth illustrates the words of Jean Cocteau:

Our era is scholarly and uncultured; everyone is a professor who knows nothing and wants to teach it to others.[2]

---

[1] Roger Dachez: "GLNF: le plus grand scandale en Europe depuis un siècle", *La Lumière, the Masonic blog of L'Express,* August 1, 2011. (http://blogs.lexpress.fr/lumiere-franc-macon/2011/08/01/roger-dachez-glnf-le-plus-grand-scandale-en-europe-depuis-un-siecle/).

[2] Jean Cocteau, *Le Passé Défini. I. 1951–1952* (Paris: Gallimard, 1983), 20.

Or those of Marcel Proust:

But one can easily twist accounts of the past which nobody knows anything more about as those of travels in countries where no one has ever been.[3]

---

[3] Marcel Proust, *Le Temps Retrouvé* (Paris: Pléiade 1989), IV, 563.

I

LANDMARKS, RECOGNITION, REGULARITY

No student can afford to be ignorant or careless of the ceaseless changes of meaning in the words of a living language. The words "Warrant," "Constitution," and "Regular" connote many things to-day which our forefathers had not in view at the Revival of 1717.

W. J. Chetwode Crawley
Cæmentaria Hibernica, Vol. 2, 1896.

LANDMARK... TWO LANDMARKS...
"FIRST LANDMARK"?

> Let's be serious! One statement only is historically and traditionally possible: no one has ever seen a landmark because, in fact , a landmark is nothing but a myth forged by a poet... .
>
> Marius Lepage[4]

The English word LAND-MARKS appeared in 1720 at the beginning of ART. XXXIX of the *General Regulations* by George Payne,[5] included in *The Constitutions of the Free-Masons*, a book published in London in 1723, the second edition of which appeared in 1738.

Anthology III

The United Grand Lodge was born in 1813, it refers to the Constitutions of Anderson of 1737 [...]

Alain BAUER, 1999[6]

Furthermore, it is strange to record that the famous articles one and two in Anderson's Constitutions *repeat verbatim corresponding articles in the Royal Society's* General Regulations *[...]*

Charles PORSET, 1999[7]

---

[4]   Marius Lepage, *L'ORDRE et les Obédiences* (Lyon, France: Paul Derain, 1956), 96.

[5]   *The Constitutions of the Free-Masons*, 1723, 70.

[6]   Alain Bauer, *De la régularité maçonnique*, edited by Alain Bauer (Paris: Éditions maçonniques de France, 1999), 16.

[7]   Charles Porset, *De la régularité maçonnique*, op. cit. 49. This "strange observation" is a

1929 Invention of Landmarks.

Alain BAUER, 2003[8]

This article became article 9 in the French *Reglemens Généraux* of 1743, in which *Landmark* is translated into French as *limites*:

> Every annual Gr. Lodge has the inherent power and authority to make new regulations or to change them for the true benefit of the brotherhood, as long as the Ancient Landmarks [Les anciennes Limites] always be carefully preserved.

In 1788, the Grand Secretary of the Ancients, writing to the Scottish Grand Master Mason, mentioned "the Deviation" of the Moderns:

> We trust the time is not far distant when, sensible of the inconvenience as well as the fault of the Deviation, they will come back within the Landmarks of the Craft.[9]

The minutes of the Lodge of Promulgation of October 19, 1810 judged that it was necessary to observe the ceremony of a Master of a Lodge, which was "one of the two *Landmarks* of the Craft". When, a century later, Hextall rediscovered this text, he did not hesitate to write that it was most certainly an error and that the word "two" should have been "true". His suggestion caused the Irishman Chetwode Crawley to respond ironically:

> Only two Landmarks were in question. The first has already been disposed of, by recognising and redressing the "Variations" in the preparatory E.A. and F.C. Degrees that stand for a Novitiate."[10]

The notion of the "first and most important landmark" seems to have appeared in the resolution dated March 6, 1878, by the United Grand Lodge of England, which we will discuss more later:

---

product of its author's imagination.

[8] Alain Bauer, *Aux origines de la franc-maçonnerie* (Paris: Dervy, 2003), 103.

[9] Charles Bolton 1897, *Grand Master's Lodge No.1*, 22, quoted in W. B. Hextall, "The Special Lodge of Promulgation," *AQC* 23 (1910): 48.

[10] Hextall, op. cit. 50. Chetwode Crawley, "The International Compact, 1814," *AQC* 28 (1915), 144.

That the Grand Lodge, whilst always anxious to receive in the most fraternal spirit the Brethren of any Foreign Grand Lodge whose proceedings are conducted according to the Ancient Landmarks of the Order, of which a belief in T. G. A. O. T. V is the first and the most important [...]

In an article published in 1952 in *Ars Quatuor Coronatorum*, F. R. Worts concluded:

Although the most "knowledgeable" Masons had a shrewd idea of what the Landmarks were, few were able to define them or justify their selection, except perhaps the First Landmark, which admittedly, was the acceptance of the G. A. O. T.U. [11]

John Rylands commented drily on this conclusion:

Even in respect of what is miscalled the First Landmark, Bro. Worts feels constrained to insert "perhaps" when discussing the subject.

In 1984, my friend Wallace McLeod emphasized the ambivalence of the word landmark:

The whole question of masonic jurisprudence is a vexed one, for while we like to believe that the essential features of the Craft are 'landmarks' and therefore not amenable to legislation, still nobody knows just what the landmarks are, and every Grand Lodge has authority to make its own laws. It takes tact to know how much change can be introduced without undermining the fundamentals. Freemasonry, from its origin to the present time, has continued to evolve, and there has never been a time when one could say, 'this is masonry at its purest'. [12]

---

[11] Frederick Roberts Worts, "The Use of the Word 'Landmarks': Deductions," *AQC* 75 (1952) and the comments it generated. See also: '*Les Landmarks*' in Daruty, 1879 *Recherches sur le Rite Écossais Ancien Accepté* (reprint, Paris: Éditions Télètes, 2002),, 28–36; Alfred Jonas Axel Poignant (a Swede who was naturalized in England in 1914), "The Landmarks," *AQC* 24 (1911); Alex Horne, "Buddhist Ideas concerning God and Immortality - A Study in Masonic Jurisprudence," *AQC* 86 (1973).

[12] Wallace McLeod commenting on Christopher Haffner's article, "Regularity of Origin," *AQC* 96 (1983): 129.

RECOGNITION

The word 'recognize' is inseparable from two sentences that have been in the French Masonic instructions since 1744:

Are you a Mason?
My Brothers & Fellows recognize me as such.[13]

They repeat the first English instructions:

SIM. And are you a Mason.
PHIL. I am (so taken to be by all Fellows and Brothers).[14]

Q. Are you a Mason?
A. I am so taken and Accepted to be amongst Brothers and Fellows.[15]

The entry *Recognition* in English Masonic encyclopedias, those of Mackey (1874) and Kenning (January 1878), is accompanied by the words "signs of" added in parentheses. At that time, the word was only used in English Masonic vocabulary in the expression "signs of recognition".

It was in March 1878 that an additional meaning was attributed to the word recognize, which is now familiar to Freemasons the world over:

That the Grand Lodge [...] cannot recognise as 'true and genuine' Brethren any who have been initiated in Lodges which either deny or ignore that belief [in a Grand Architect of the Universe].

---

[13] *Catechisme des Franc-Maçons* (1744), *L'Ordre des Francs-Macons trahi* (1745), *Le Sceau Rompu* (1745).
[14] *A Dialogue between Simon, a Town Mason, & Philip, a traveling Mason* (~1725).
[16] *Masonry Dissected* (1730).

Recognition reappeared in *Basic Principles for Grand Lodge Recognition* (1929) and *Aims and Relationships of the Craft* (1938), two texts cited in the appendix and discussed later.

REGULAR AND REGULARITY
LONDON, EDINBURGH, PARIS

When the word regular was used in the eighteenth century in a Masonic context, it had the same meaning in Great Britain and France: a lodge is regular once it has received a constitution from the Grand Master of the obedience to which it seeks to be related. It appears in the *General Regulations* by Grand Master George Payne, which was included in *The Constitutions of the Freemason* in 1723. The end of article VIII of the *General Regulations*,

> If any Set or Number of Masons shall take upon themselves to form a Lodge without the Grand-Master's Warrant, *the* regular Lodges are not to countenance them, nor own them as fair Brethren and duly form'd, nor approve of their Acts and Deeds;

is repeated word for word at the beginning of article 16 of the General Regulations adopted by the grand lodge assembled in Paris on December 11, 1743[16]:

> If any Masons take it upon themselves to form a Lodge without the G. M.'s permission, the regular Lodges are not to countenance them nor own them as honorable brethren and duly formed; they must also not approve their acts and deeds..

On October 15, 1736, in Edinburgh, six weeks before the election of the first Grand Master Mason, William St. Clair, a committee from four lodges wrote a decree addressed to "all the

---

[16] This remark, which I made in an article published in the Masonic magazone *Alpina* in 1999 and repeated on p. 43 in *Une certaine idée de la franc-maçonnerie* (Paris: Dervy, 2008), is recopied in Michel Barat, Alain Bauer, and Roger Dachez, *Les promesses de l'aube* (Paris: Dervy, 2013), 29.

known regular lodges in Scotland". The discussion at the Grand Lodge on the following November 30 shows that the word could also be understood as applying to the regular intervals between its meetings.[17]

In 1751, when Irish Freemasons gathered in a General Assembly in London, they used the word regular without defining it according to art. 6 of their *Rules* approved on July 17:

> THAT no Old Mason shall be admitted a Member of any Lodge unless he hath been made in a Regular Lodge [...].

---

[17] Robert Strathern Lindsay, *A History of the Mason Lodge of Holyrood House (St Luke's) N° 44* (Edinburgh: University Press, 1935), 48–58.

II

THE GRAND ORIENT OF FRANCE FROM 1773 TO 1877

> *Bro∴ Pillot, head of the Secretariat, ended his presentation of the Report on the Proceedings of the G∴ O∴ during the year 5848 with these words*: "Like God from whom it emanates, *Freemasonry is immortal.*"
>
> Grand Orient Bulletin (March 1849): 270.

1773 AND AFTER

In 1773 in Paris, the first chapter of the *Statuts de l'Ordre Royal de la Franc-Maçonnerie en France*, ratified, finalized, and signed on Saturday, April 17 during the sixth assembly of the National Grand Lodge of France, defined the word regular without any hint of ambiguity:

Article I.

The Body of the Royal Order of Freemasonry under the distinguished title of *Masonic Body of France*, shall only be composed of Regular Masons, recognized as such by the Grand Orient.

Art. II.

The Grand Orient of France shall from this point only recognize as *Regular Masons* those who are Members of Regular Lodges.

Art. III.

The Grand Orient of France shall from this point only recognize as Regular Lodges those with Constitutions given or renewed by it; & it only shall have the right to issue them.[18]

Anthology III

Let us therefore cease from rewriting history as the now defunct Soviet Encyclopedia used to do, depending on the whims or fantasies of the Supreme

---

[18] Transcription based on the original. Groussier's transcription, "to deliberate them", in *Constitution du Grand Orient de France par la Grande Loge Nationale 1773* (Paris: Gloton, 1931), [231], is wrong.

Soviet[...] In 1773, during the assembly of all the lodges at the Grand Orient, it was decided that a lodge was regular when it was made up of seven regular Freemasons. A pragmatism that has unfortunately been forgotten.

Alain BAUER[19]

The Grand Orient maintained the same definitions in its *Statutes and General Regulations* for more than a century:

1839

Irregular Masons are: 1° Any Profane received as Mason in a Lodge not recognized by the G∴ O∴, or by a Mason who is not qualified to confer this title; (art. 203).

1867, 1873, 1882

Any Mason, to be regular, must either be an active member of a regular Lodge [...] or an honorary member (art. 155). Irregular masons are: 1° Any profane initiated in a Lodge not recognized by the Grand Orient or anywhere else than in a regular Lodge; (art. 162).

Along two centuries, regular lodges are those that received authorization from the Grand Master or Warrants of the Grand Lodge to which they belong. Regular Freemasons are those who belong to a regular lodge.

---

[19] Alain Bauer, *Le crépuscule des frères La fin de la franc-maçonnerie?* (Paris: La Table Ronde, 2006), 45 and 78.

1839

The new edition (1838) of the *Statutes and General Regulations of the Masonic Order in France* is preceded by a *Summary of Reports made to the G∴ O∴ of France for the Revision Committee.*[20] The rapporteur, Pierre-Gérard Vassal, writes:

> In fact, we can see, by going back to the origin of our institution in France, that at that time it had no written laws and that habit or traditions that changed to varying degrees over time were the only compass to serve as rules for the founders of this fraternal and philanthropic Association, until the time when the G∴ O∴ lay the first organic foundations of the Order in harmony with the principles upon which it rests [...]. The only rules these early meetings had were the ritual for each degree; any jurisdiction and arbiter were simply based on the will and good pleasure of each W. M. [...]. the presidents of the Lodges of the capital met [...] on December 11, 1743, under the name of English G∴ L∴ of France [...]

In other words, the members of the Committee were ignorant of the existence of texts earlier than the Statutes of 1773[21] and Vassal was repeating an imaginary statement by Thory.[22]

Nothing was added or modified in 1838 to the provisions that had been adopted at the beginning of the *Statutes* of 1826, except for the minimum age to become a mason: it was now sufficient to be eighteen years old and have the consent of one's father or guardian.

---

[20] *Statuts et Réglemens Généraux de l'Ordre Maçonnique en France* (Paris: Imprimerie de Veuve Dondey-Dupré, 5839), v-xxviii.

[21] Les *Statuts de l'Ordre* of 1763 were published by Arthur Groussier (*Documents relatifs à l'Histoire du G. O. D. F.*, July 1929). I published the *Règlemens Généraux* of 1743 in vol. x (1974) of *Travaux de Villard de Honnecourt*.

[22] Thory, *Acta Latomorum* (Paris: Dufart, 1815 [Paris: Slatkine Reprints, 1980]), I, 53.

1849 THE GRAND ORIENT ADOPTS A CONSTITUTION

On January 14, 1848, the Grand Orient's special session heard a report from its Permanent Committee on the following question: *How can the distinctive religious nature of Freemasonry be restored*?

Brother Blanchet, former Worshipful Master of *Les Neuf Sœurs*, is the author of this report whose title, but not the text, went down in history. Jouaust cited it at length in order to criticize it:

> Please do not speak to the rapporteur of the Permanent Committee of the utopias of Masonic progress, because he is its sworn enemy: "Often we have been told that Freemasonry's duty was to be at the forefront of progress, and to take initiative in the social movement; people have said that if your Institution is threatened with ruin, it was no doubt due to having failed in this mission and to have moved away from the secular world. A thoughtless reproach! An ambitious claim, which if it succeeded would be disastrous for us! To put ourselves at the forefront of the social movement, we would have to have the strength to guide it towards a moral goal; and we do not have such strength; and the current movement would push us towards a goal that is diametrically opposed to what we are proposing [...]"

> We leave it to the common sense of our readers to determine the real value of these commonplaces concerning morals, these odd reasonings concerning the goal of Masonry, these contradictions and philosophical nonsense, which precede a no less curious draft decree: "The G. O., considering that the nature of Freemasonry is essentially religious... — Considering that, for some time, this religious nature seems to have weakened, this is due no doubt to the invasion of secular passions [...]"

> Certain documents depict the tendencies of an era or a party better than any reflections by a historian, and we believe that every word of this incredible project should be viewed as an example of the intellectual decrepitude of one

part of the Grand Orient in 1848; for praises were lavished upon this misguided work, read during a special session of the Grand Orient [...]

The discussion was summarized by establishing that Freemasonry is truly a religion, but a religion which, in its moral doctrine, includes all of them and excludes none, accepting above all Divinity as its belief; that it corresponds to a philosophical authority, without which there would be no worship, no belief, and which is itself a religion; that this philosophy, which is that of humankind, moves forward with the centuries and cannot be stopped; that this here is Freemasonry's philosophy, according to which we may establish its truly religious nature [...].

The execution of the misguided project was hastily buried by sending it back to the Statutes Review Committee; but one had the lack of intelligence of granting it the honor of the official Bulletin, where it will now remain as an immortal monument to the weak Masonic principles of the leading body of French Freemasonry.[23]

During the following August, the committee responsible for drafting the Constitution, which the Grand Orient of France decided to adopt for the first time in its history, included a third article, which in the end would not be retained. The text was as follows:

Masonry recognizes and proclaims, as the starting point for its philosophical research and as facts beyond any contention, the existence of God and the immortality of the soul.[24]

Anthology IV

For its part, article 3 of the Constitutions recalls the requirement to believe and the text shows [sic] that "Freemasonry knows and proclaims, as the starting point for its philosophical research and as fact beyond any contention, the existence of God."

Pierre-Yves BEAUREPAIRE, 2000[25]

---

[23] A.G. Jouaust, *Histoire du Grand-Orient de France* (Rennes: Leroy, 1865. Facsimile reprint. Paris: Télètes, 1989, 495–501.

[24] Pierre Chevallier, *Histoire de la Franc-Maçonnerie française,* vol. 2 (Paris: Fayard, 1974), 336.

[25] Pierre-Yves Beaurepaire (*Encyclopédie de la Franc-Maçonnerie,* edited by Éric Saunier, Paris: La Pochotèque, 2000), 354), recopied Pierre Chevallier (note 24 *supra*) without citing his source and misunderstood the meaning.

The Constitution finally ratified by the General Assembly on August 10, 1849[26] begins with the following 1st article:

> Freemasonry, an essentially philanthropic, philosophical, and progressive institution, has as its base the existence of God and the immortality of the soul; its goal is to exercise charity, study universal morality, arts, and sciences, and to practice all virtues. Its motto has always been: Liberty, Equality, Fraternity.[27]

In the *Survey* "of the various Constitutions and General Statutes that followed the General Statutes of 1839" he had "gathered and offered to b. Du Hamel on March 1, 1876", Bro. Thévenot, head of the Secretariat of the Grand Orient of France since 1855, added the following handwritten note next to the *Constitution of 1849*: "Was not put into practice."[28]

Anthology V

Article 1 of the Constitution of the Grand Orient of France, written in 1949 [sic], *indicates that:* "Freemasonry, an essentially philanthropic, philosophical, and progressive institution, has as its base the existence of God and the immortality of the soul."

Jean-Michel Ducomte, 1999[29]

But in 1849, there was a change in tone. The Grand Orient introduced into its constitution the obligatory recognition [sic] *of the existence of God* [...]

Alain Bauer, 2010[30]

---

26 Not "April 13, 1849", Alain Bauer and Edouard Boeglin, *Le Grand Orient de France* (Paris: Presses universitaires de France, 2002), 43.

27 Text of the Duez amendement (Adrien Juvanon 1926, *Vers la lumière* (Paris: Imprimerie Centrale de la Bourse, 1926), 37). The last sentence, which Robert Amadou qualified humorously as a "historical blunder" (*Renaissance Traditionnelle* 21–22 (1975): 31) disappeared in the 1854 revision but reappeared in 1865.

28 Alain Bernheim Archives.

29 J.-M. Ducompte (then Grand Secretary for External Affairs for Grand Master Alain Bauer), *De la Régularité maçonnique*, 89.

30 Alain Bauer, *Dictionnaire amoureux de la Franc-Maçonnerie* (Paris: Plon, 2010), under the entry *Croire ou ne pas croire* [To believe or not to believe].

FROM 1849 TO 1865

During this period, almost all General Assemblies of the Grand Orient criticized the 1st article of 1849 or offered proposals to amend it. It was modified by the Convent in General Assembly on October 28, 1854:

> The Order of Freemasons has as its purpose charity, the study of universal morality, and the practice of all virtues. It has as its base: the existence of God, the immortality of the soul, and the love of humanity. It is composed of free men who, subject to the laws, gather in a Society governed by general and particular Statutes.

During the Convent of June 1865, Brother Thelmier declared:

> In the midst of such differing opinions, it is difficult to be conciliatory. I have nonetheless sought to be, and please tell me if I have succeeded. I belong to those who do not seek to fully inscribe the name of God and the immortality of the soul into the Constitution; however, on the frontispiece of this Constitution, I set an important word that governed Freemasonry until 1849, which has been with us since the beginning, and this is that of the Grand Architect of the Universe; it is under this invocation that I place the principles of Freemasonry. Why would we inscribe words into the Constitution that divide us, that may make us intolerant? Based on this logic, we should put out of the temple those who present themselves to us and say "I doubt", as a Brother has observed. Leave to each his own inspiration. I would keep the words grand architect, which meet any possible aspiration, all desires. For Mohammedans, it is Allah; for Christians, it is the entire Trinity; for the Hindus, it is Brahma or Shiva; for us, it is God; for those who doubt, it is the intelligent formula of laws that govern the universe.[31]

Article 1 was then modified again:

---

[31]   Juvanon 1926, *Vers la lumière*, 40.

Freemasonry, an essentially philanthropic, philosophical, and progressive institution, has as its purpose the search for truth, the study of universal morality, arts, and sciences, and the exercise of charity. Its principles are the existence of God, the immortality of the soul and human solidarity. It considers liberty of conscience as a right unique to each man and excludes no one for his beliefs. Its motto is: Liberty, Equality, Fraternity.

The final modification, which would lead to the setting aside of the Grand Orient of France from 1878 until today, resulted from a very brief resolution presented to the Convent of 1875 by a small provincial lodge, *La Fraternité progressive*, Orient from Villefranche (Rhône):

Delete the first two terms of the second paragraph from the first article of the Constitution.

THE COUNCIL OF THE ORDER'S MEETING JULY 1876

Brother Du Hamel read a report on the subject of the resolution by the Villefranche lodge at the Council of the Order's meeting on July 29, 1876. After recalling the numerous similar resolutions submitted to the Council since 1868, Du Hamel announced:

> Today, as at these other times, you will think, as I do, that this resolution, by eliminating the traditional phrase found in the entire Masonic world, eliminates article 1 of our Constitution; modifies completely the principles governing our Institution and which, in the very terms of these principles, represent its foundations. If such a modification were to be made to our Constitution, no one could deny that, apart from the attacks of the secular world which do not concern me, for the elimination of this phrase does not in itself result in the negation of God, we would be governed by the theory of independent morality. It will therefore be up to us to see, were the question to present itself one day before the Assembly, whether we want to change the foundation of our institution [...].[32]

The Council then moved on to the agenda.

---

[32] *Bulletin du Grand Orient* (1876): 185-186.

THE CONVENT OF SEPTEMBER 1876

The resolution came before the Convent on September 14. As soon as the rapporteur of the Committee of Resolutions, Bro. Massicault, began to speak, the matter seems to have been accepted:

> Your committee, my Brethren, was almost unanimous on several points. It first recognized that only bad faith could liken the elimination requested to a negation of the existence of God and the immortality of the soul; for human solidarity and liberty of conscience, which would then be the exclusive foundations of Freemasonry, certainly include belief in God and an immortal soul, as well as they allow for materialism, positivism, or any other philosophical doctrine.[33]

The Committee for whom he was speaking proposed, by a vote of 5 to 4 to move on to the agenda, because the effect of this reform

> would be to provoke ardent controversies, inevitable ferments of discord, in almost all Lodges, and it would have disastrous repercussions in the secular world [...]. [Circumstances] deter us from compromising our relations with foreign Masonic powers, from troubling our fraternal harmony [...].

An intervention from Brother Nesme, W. M. of the Villefranche Lodge which issued the resolution, clarified the situation:

> What caused this idea [the resolution made by his lodge] to arise, was a matter that occurred in our Lodge, when we received two candidates: one believed in the existence of the Supreme Being, the other did not. When they underwent the tests and answered the questions they were asked, the neophytes withdrew as usual, so that the Brethren present could discuss their answers. One Brother asked to speak, noting that one of them did not believe

---

[33]   *Bulletin du Grand Orient* (1876), 373.

in the existence of the Supreme Being, and that our Constitution had as one of its principles the existence of the Supreme Being and the immortality of the soul. We had to indicate to this Brother that art. 2 of the Constitution respects religious faith, and as a result, all beliefs. It is true that it is possible to have as a religion the religion of reason, of not harming anyone and seeking to do good, according to our means. This religion has not yet become a matter of worship, it is true; but it is the liberty of conscience to which every Freemason must lay claim. We believed that by removing the 1st § from art. 1 of the Constitution, you would prevent many unpleasant discussions on a question about which we are somewhat divided, that is, about which we differ in belief.[34]

This led the rapporteur to declare:

This is, Brethren, the incident that led to this debate. And really, it's hard to believe that for an event like this, we would change our Statutes, consult the Lodges, and upset the established way of operating!

André Rousselle, an "activist atheist" and one of the leaders of *Monde Maçonnique*,[35] said then:

I am therefore not surprised by the objection I have encountered before me today. It rises up before all innovators. In the past, this was called respecting tradition but today is called opportunism.[...] You first spoke of the false and untrue interpretation other foreign Grand Orients may make concerning our vote, and which may perhaps result in the isolation of French Freemasonry within universal Freemasonry. Your assumptions hardly have any bearing, because they are purely unwarranted and are not based on any foundation.

However, Nicoullaud, from the *Pyramides* lodge of Alexandria said:

[...] we admire the wonders that nature and science set before us; this is the way in which the progress made brings us closer and closer to God each day, by revealing to us the laws of creation [...] But in order for Freemasonry to play a role in greatly improving social relations, for it to exercise a positive influence and sustainable action, it must realize that while there are necessary freedoms, there are also necessary ideas; it must maintain the idea, throughout all the doctrines, that is at the peak of all religions, almost all philosophies, and, whether one believes it or not, in the depths of all consciousness: the idea of God!

And Nicoullaud recalled a few circumstances that surrounded Abd-el-Kader's initiation who, in his answers, declared at the moment of his initiation:

---

[34] *Bulletin du Grand Orient* (1876): 376–377.
[35] Jean Baylot, *La voie substituée* (Liège, Belgium: Éditions Borp S.A., 1968), 319.

"Would I be a real believer if I did not accept your principles, if I did not practice your virtues? Do we not have the same God?" Well! I can attest that if Freemasonry had not been presented to him with the principles inscribed in its Constitution, we would not be able to include this illustrious man among the members of our Order.

One of the arguments then put forward by Bro. Berr demonstrates the atmosphere permeating certain lodges:

A profane presents himself: reports are excellent [...] accordingly he is unanimously accepted to undergo the Masonic tests. During the questions posed to him, he is asked whether he has ever prayed. Upon his response that during difficult times in his life, he has sometimes offered prayers to the Supreme Being, he is rewarded with 27 black balls, and his initiation is rejected![36]

Dr. Eugène Marchal, W. M. of *St Jeande Jérusalem* in Nancy and member of the Council of the Order, then spoke:

[...] we have neglected to say that the resolution is in direct opposition to the solidarity which ties the Grand Orient of France to foreign Grand Orients and which is based on a community of principles that would disappear if we eliminated the paragraph in question and the phrase *Grand Architect of Worlds*; do not believe, my Brethren, that the paragraph discussed and this phrase are simply vain words: these are eternal ideas that have gone through the centuries and based upon which innumerable civilizations have been raised up; these are the same ideas that inspired the first founders of Freemasonry and the writers of our rituals, and everything has been built upon them. They are the cornerstone, and we are seeking to remove it, which if it were to happen, the Temple would instantly collapse and we would find ourselves in ruins, which would be the end of Freemasonry. We could do something else, something new, I agree, but it would no longer be Freemasonry. And then, since this is what we belong to, we would have to leave the Grand Orient of France and go practice it elsewhere.[37]

In his response to the speakers, the rapporteur said very clearly:

No doubt, if you accept the resolution, it would not be true that you had established a dogma of the negation of God's existence and the immortality of the soul. The Report and discussion of today would stand in vigorous protest against such slander. But you would not impede our adversaries from making such a claim [...].

Closure was then requested, and the Assembly was preparing to vote on the report's conclusions when Rousselle presented an

---

[36] *Bulletin du Grand Orient* (1876): 393–394.
[37] *Bulletin du Grand Orient* (1876): 400–401.

agenda item. It was to first vote on the report by the Resolutions Committee, which wanted an up-or-down vote on the agenda item. By a vote of 110 to 65, the report was rejected.[38] As a result, the resolution presented by the Villefranche lodge was sent back to the lodges for further study.

We need also to examine the publication of an article in *Le Monde Maçonnique* dated July 1877 by Jean Marie Caubet, who was the editor. Baylot writes that he was Councilor of the Order for more than ten years, W. M. of his Lodge, *La Rose du Parfait Silence*, since 1856, a bookseller, the least cultured of those nicknamed by Baylot the Conquerors (together with Massol, Fauvety, Guépin and Riche Gardon), and that the National Library has preserved his "secularized catechisms of the three degrees that attest to his specific ignorance."[39]

The best illustration of these harsh words can be found in Caubet:

> Everyone knows today that the terms to be deleted were only introduced for the first time into our declarations of principles in 1849. Therefore, in this situation, tradition is on our side and against those who invoked it too wantonly [...]. In a progressive association, the role of tradition is moreover, very secondary [...]. It should not [...] have the least influence on our actions when it goes against the law of progress. But let us say again, on this occasion, tradition is fully for us. We should add that the importance still ascribed today in our regulations to the motto: To the Glory of the Grand Architect of the Universe originated first after 1849.[40]

[38] *Bulletin du Grand Orient* (1876): 407–410 with the names of the voters.
[39] Baylot, *La voie substituée*, 366–368.
[40] *Le Monde Maçonnique* (July 1877): 117–121.

THE CONVENT OF SEPTEMBER 1877

A nine-member committee was appointed concerning Villefranche's resolution in the second session. Grand Master de Saint Jean declared clearly that he was against the resolution. The discussion took place on Thursday, the 13th, and the rapporteur was minister Frédéric Desmons. His speech has been quoted many times.[41] It contains hardly any new elements compared to what occurred during the Convent of 1876. Desmons raised objections to the three main arguments presented by the opponents of the resolution he reported, that is, that it risked "isolating [the Grand Orient] within universal Masonry, creating troublesome unrest in our Lodges, and provoking a regrettable schism within the Grand Orient of France, which the declared enemies of our Grand Orient would take advantage of to slander all Masons, by denouncing them in the secular world as materialists or atheists." He was careful not to mention the objection that the Councilor of the Order Du Hamel had raised the previous year: the adoption of this resolution would result in completely modifying the principles that govern our Institution and which, in the very terms of these principles, serve as its foundation. But Desmons was right in declaring:

> Let us leave discussions concerning dogma to the theologians [...]. May it [Freemasonry] never descend into the fiery arena of theological discussions

---

[41] Juvanon 1926, *Vers la lumière*, 53–60. *Bulletin du Centre de Documentation du Grand Orient de France* 11–12 (1958): 46–54. Daniel Ligou, *Frédéric Desmons et la Franc-Maçonnerie sous la 3ᵉ République* (1966), 86–92.

[...] May Freemasonry rise therefore majestically above any questions of Churches or sects [...].

The resolution by the Villefranche lodge was adopted by standing by a large majority.[42] Article 1 of the Constitution of the Grand Orient of France then became:

Freemasonry, an essentially philanthropic, philosophical, and progressive institution, has as its purpose the search for truth, the study of universal morality, arts, and sciences, and the exercise of charity. Its principles are the absolute liberty of conscience and human solidarity. It excludes no person due to his beliefs. Its motto is: "Liberty, Equality, Fraternity."

Desmons makes no mention at all of the Grand Architect of the Universe in his famous report, and no decision by the Convent of 1877 mentions it.[43]

Anthology VI

Pastor Desmons who was the prime mover of the changes, gave wholehearted support for the expulsion of the Grand Architect from French Freemasonry.[44]

How in his soul and conscience could pastor Frédéric Desmons exclaim "We ask for the deletion of this phrase (the reference to the Grand Architect of the Universe) because it seems to us to be completely useless and foreign to the goal of Masonry."[45]

Michel BRODSKY 1993 and 1998

[...] if we are to believe the Masons of the United Grand Lodge of England and their continental followers, the Grand Orient excluded itself from

---

[42]   Ligou 1966, 93 in a note, quoting the *Bulletin du Grand Orient* (1900): 359, mentions that during the Convent of 1900 Desmons confirmed that it was unanimous less three votes.

[43]   Henri Amblaine [Alain Bernheim], "La Franc-Maçonnerie, l'Angleterre et les mythes," *Acta Macionica* 9 (1999): 371. Pierre Noël, "Le Convent de 1877..." *Acta Macionica* 10 (2000): 316.

[44]   Michel Brodsky, "The Regular Freemason," *AQC* 106 (1993): 111.

[45]   Michel Brodsky, "Le convent du Grand Orient de France de 1877," *Acta Macionica* 8 (1998): 349. The words in parentheses in the quotation were added by Michel Brodsky and are not found in the report by pastor Desmons.

universal Masonry in 1877 when in the course of a memorable convent it decided to eliminate from its Constitutions the obligation (introduced in 1849) to believe in a revealed principle and the immortality of the soul.

Charles PORSET, 1999 [46]

The year 1865 was an occasion for a fundamental debate which only really concluded in 1877 with the disappearance of the required reference to the Grand Architect of the Universe in the constitutional texts. ... elimination of the Grand Architect in 1877... The Grand Orient thus took leave of the Grand Architect.

Alain BAUER and Edouard BOEGLIN, 2003 [47]

...in 1877... the decision took hold without any issue and the resolution was adopted by a large majority, at the proposal of the president of the Council of the Order, pastor Frédéric Desmons.

Roger DACHEZ and Alain BAUER, 2013 [48]

---

[46] Charles Porset, "De la régularité en maçonnerie. Notes d'histoire," in *De la Régularité maçonnique*, 45.

[47] Bauer and Boeglin, *Le Grand Orient de France*, 48, 49, and 56.

[48] Roger Dachez and Alain Bauer, *La Franc-Maçonnerie* (Paris: Presses universitaires de France, 2013), 44. Pastor Desmons had been a member of the Council of the Order several times since 1873. He became its Chairman for the first time in 1887 (Ligou 1966, 75–76, 117, 123, 131, 133) after having resigned as pastor in 1881 (Ligou 1966, 102–103).

III

INTERNATIONAL RELATIONS IN THE NINETEENTH CENTURY

Pierre Chevallier reported on the visit of two members of the Council of the Grand Master during the Great Exhibition held in London in 1851. The response they received was "that because the United Lodge does not recognize High Degrees, it did not have to maintain relations with an authority claiming these degrees, which it regarded and declared as foreign to the only true Freemasonry, that of the Symbolic Degrees."[49]

---

[49] Chevallier, *Histoire de la franc-maçonnerie française*, 374 (see Emmanuel Rebold, *Histoire des trois Grandes Loges* (Paris: Collignon, 1864), 276, note 3). Recent research has revealed the difficulties encountered during the creation of the United Grand Lodge of England in 1813 (Alain Bernheim, "England, Scotland, Ireland and the International Compact of 1814," *The Square* (June 2013): 19–22. John Belton, "The 1814 International Compact and 'Pure Ancient Masonry,'" *The Square* (September 2014): 21-22). The oldest document in the archives of the Supreme Council for England and Wales (founded by patent backdated to October 26, 1845) showing a relationship with the United Grand Lodge is dated January 11, (John Mandleberg, *Ancient and Accepted*, Published in 1995 for The Supreme Council 33°), 185.

THE CONVENT OF THE SUPREME COUNCILS OF THE ANCIENT AND ACCEPTED SCOTTISH RITE[50]

Six Supreme Councils were present in Lausanne on September 6, 1875: England, Belgium, Colon (Cuba), France, Italy, and Switzerland (the Supreme Councils of Hungary, Peru, and Portugal gave the Supreme Council of Switzerland proxy to represent them). There was also a delegate from the Supreme Council of Scotland, Lindsay Mackersy, who decided to leave Lausanne on the 8th after the committee meeting that was responsible for preparing the terms for a *Declaration of Principles*.

Among the texts approved by the Convent after being discussed in committee, the *Treaty of Masonic Union, Alliance, and Confederation* included a *Declaration of Principles* that was published separately with the title *Manifest of the Convent of Lausanne*. Its drafting had been entrusted to the Very Illustrious Brethren Crémieux (Grand Commander of the Supreme Council of France), Besançon (Grand Commander of the Supreme Council of Switzerland) and Montagu (Grand Chancellor of the Supreme Council for England and Wales). Adopted on September 22 and made public after the work done at the Convent, the *Manifest* opened with the following words:

---

[50] This Convent and its results are described in Alain Bernheim, *Le rite en 33 grades. De Frederick Dalcho à Charles Riandey* (Paris: Dervy, 2011), 371–439 and 572–587.

41

> Freemasonry proclaims, as it has proclaimed since its origin, the existence of a creative principle under the name of Grand Architect of the Universe.

At the meeting of October 12, the English Supreme Council listened to one of its three delegates, Hugh David Sandman, present a summary of his report and provide the English translation of the texts adopted in Lausanne. The Supreme Council ratified the action of its delegates.[51]

For various reasons, there followed a series of splits and reconciliations between Supreme Councils: The split of the Grand Orient of France with the Supreme Council of France in 1875, of the Southern Jurisdiction of the United States with the Supreme Council of France the same year, the split of England with Scotland on November 26, 1877 (England decided then to eliminate the word Scottish from the expression Ancient and Accepted Scottish Rite), followed by their reconciliation in 1889, and the restoration of official relations between the Southern Jurisdiction and the Supreme Council of France in 1890.

---

[51] Mandleberg, *Ancient and Accepted*, 277. Bernheim, *Le rite en 33 grades*, 399–401.

FRANCE

John Hamill recalled the three different positions adopted by our English Brethren during the nineteenth century with regard to their international relations: the refusal to establish relations; an intermediary position characterized by the authorization of mutual visits and by the existence of correspondence between the Grand Secretaries; and the exchange of Representatives, which in French are called *Garants d'Amitié*.[52] In 1875, the Grand Orient of France had a Representative in the Grand Lodge of Scotland, Brother Loth.[53] There was also one in the Grand Lodge of Ireland, Deputy Grand Master Edward Borough.

On March 29, 1875, Antoine de Saint-Jean, President of the Council of the Order, wrote on behalf of the Grand Orient to H.R.H. Albert Edward, 23rd Prince of Wales and future Edward VII[54]:

> The entire Masonic world welcomed your accession to the Grand Mastery of the Order, in England, as an event that history will remember as among the most pleasing for Freemasonry. The Grand Orient of France, like all Masonic Powers on the Globe applauded this event; and, in the chorus of congratulations addressed to Your Highness, it is our duty to convey those of French Freemasonry as well [...]. May our fraternal approach please you and contribute to bringing the relations between the two Obediences of England and France closer together, two sisters already united by the same aspirations and the goal they are both pursuing with equal vigor.

Grand Secretary John Hervey answered on May 18:

---

[52] John Hamill, commenting Brodsky's paper, *AQC* 100 (1987): 72.
[53] *Bulletin du Grand Orient* (1875): 174.
[54] *Bulletin du Grand Orient* (1875): 173–174.

I have been charged by His Royal Highness the Prince of Wales to announce that he was very pleased to receive the letter you so kindly wrote to him [...]. Please accept [...] his warmest expressions of gratitude and present them also to the Grand Orient over which you so nobly preside.

H. R. H. the Prince of Wales sincerely hopes that the same good relations which have for so long existed between the two nations will characterize the Grand Lodges of France and England, and that they will continue to pursue the same goal, which is peace on earth, charity among men, and mutual love.

BELGIUM

In 1872 the Grand Orient of Belgium – let us not forget it was then the only Grand Lodge in the country – after several years of deliberation and three days dedicated to this issue, accepted an important project:

> « The project's foreword was recalled by the Grand Orator before it was unanimously accepted.
>
> This foreword stated that « *the revision Committee judged it necessary to substitute the new phrase « The Grand Orient of Belgium decides » for the Grand Architect of the Universe »*, *a change that satisfied its legitimate aspirations* ».
>
> Art. 29 was unanimously accepted. It provided that *The Proceedings Issuing from the GO of Belgium have the following inscription in the header: In the name of the Grand Orient of Belgium.*
>
> A few secondary points were put off until later and examined in October 1871 and January 1872.
>
> The new Statutes were transcribed into the Book of Architecture on this last date.[55]
>
> [...]
>
> Rather paradoxically, the 1872 decision did not affect relations (or rather the almost total absence of relations) with England.[56]

Yet this project's adoption was followed by England's recognition of the Grand Orient of Belgium.

---

[55] Pierre Noël, "Le Grand Orient de Belgique et la mort lente du Grand Architecte de l'Univers," *Acta Macionica* 17 (2007), 408 [quotation marks and italicized words as in the paper].

[56] Noël, *ibid.*, 413.

After I had the opportunity to consult the English archives, in 1987 I published the correspondence between Grand Secretary John Harvey and Belgian Grand Master Henri Bergé, which comprises the letter Harvey sent on May 21, 1875 to the Grand Orient of Belgium, informing it of the desire of the United Grand Lodge of England to establish official relations with it and Bergé's response the following June 13.[57]

---

[57]   Alain Bernheim, commenting Brodsky's paper, *AQC* 100 (1987), 79.

THE SPLIT WITH IRELAND

Edward Borough sent a letter to the Grand Orient that was read during the meeting of the Council of the Order on November 24, 1877. In it he declared he was "renouncing his functions and the title of representative of the Grand Orient of France to the Grand Lodge of Ireland, since he was in agreement with this Masonic power which had decided to break off its relations with the G∴ O∴ of France following the changes it made to its Constitution."[58] The Chairman of the Council of the Order, from Saint-Jean, replied on November 28, 1877[59]:

> By acknowledging your resignation, Very Illustrious Brother, we cannot help but express our surprise and regret for the speed at which the Grand Lodge of Ireland has acted in this situation, [...] it was difficult to accept such an act of intolerance on the part of a Masonic Power with which the Grand Orient of France has held fraternal relations for so long [...].

> Allow me to affirm that by modifying one article of its Statutes [...], the Grand Orient of France was not seeking to make a profession of atheism, or materialism, which some seem to believe. Nothing has changed in the principles or practices of Masonry. French Freemasonry remains what it has always been, a fraternal and tolerant Masonry. Out of respect for the religious faith and political convictions of its followers, it leaves to each person, with regard to these delicate questions, the liberty of conscience [...].

> To conclude, Very Illustrious Brother, we very sincerely wish that the misunderstanding that has led you to resign from your functions as Representative of the Grand Orient of France will be dispelled, and that you would again allow us to entrust you with this mandate at the Grand Lodge of Ireland.

---

[58] Summary by Juvanon 1926, *Vers la lumière*, 60.
[59] *Le Monde Maçonnique* (January-February 1878), 390–392.

THE UNITED GRAND LODGE OF ENGLAND

During the meeting of the United Grand Lodge of England on December 15, 1877, a committee whose rapporteur was Lord Carnarvon, Pro Grand Master, was appointed to examine "the recent act of the Grand Orient of France." His draft resolution, accepted in committee on February 22,[60] was also unanimously accepted without discussion on March 6, 1878 during the quarterly meeting of the United Grand Lodge of England:

> That the Grand Lodge, whilst always anxious to receive in the most fraternal spirit the Brethren of any Foreign Grand Lodge whose proceedings are conducted according to the Ancient Landmarks of the Order, of which a belief in T. G. A. O. T. V is the first and the most important, cannot recognise as 'true and genuine' Brethren any who have been initiated in Lodges which either deny or ignore that belief.[61]

One should notice the words: cannot recognise.

---

[60]   Oswald Wirth, *Le Symbolisme*, April 1935. Quoted in Oswald Wirth, *Qui est régulier?* (Paris: Éditions du Symbolisme, 1938), 126–127.
[61]   Gould, *The History of Freemasonry*, 1882–1887, III, 26.

CAUBET'S ARTICLE

The comments that accompanied Lord Carnarvon's report have not been reproduced in French since an article by Caubet that came out the following April.[62] They are surprisingly topical for 2014:

> After having read this report, Brother Carnarvon, rapporteur, explained the scope of these resolutions and insisted they be accepted.
>
> The first resolution, he said, expressed the deep regret with which the Grand Lodge learned of the change made by the Grand Orient to its Constitution. In this matter, I believe the Grand Lodge will not deviate.
>
> The second resolution is the corollary to the first. It establishes that we cannot recognize those who took part in this change. It declares positively that there is on our side no decline in fraternal[63] feelings; it implies that we do not wish to intervene in the domain of a foreign Grand Lodge, but it means that, because the belief in the existence of the Grand Architect of the Universe is one of the principles upon which Freemasonry is founded, we cannot accept an express negation of this principle, and we cannot recognize those who deny it. I believe there will be no objection to this second resolution.
>
> If such is the case, the third is simply putting into practice the other two. The Grand Lodge should not be content with a purely theoretical and sterile declaration: this would be unworthy of it... Thus, the committee believes, and I too believe, that the Grand Lodge must not fail in its duty, as unpleasant as it is, to prescribe and determine the practical means for executing this declaration.
>
> The committee recommends that you adopt the following approach: When a foreign Brother presents himself to a Lodge to be admitted, he will be asked to produce his diploma, as is the case today, or to have a guarantor. In this regard, nothing has changed from what now exists; but we are taking a further step and are saying that the diploma must have proof that the Brother

---

[62] *Le Monde Maçonnique* (April 1878): 510–519.
[63] Note by Caubet: "The report by *The Freemason* said *paternel*. This is obviously a mistake."

was initiated in a Lodge where belief in the existence of the Supreme Architect of the Universe is required, or else (in the absence of a diploma) that some trustworthy member present must attest that the foreign Brother in question was initiated in this way.

Such is the first condition, which is necessary if you want your declaration to have a practical effect. But the committee has gone yet further; in the irregular and difficult situation the act by the Grand Orient of France has created, and given that the majority of Lodges existed before this change was made, it could be that a visitor was initiated prior to this change, and that others may have been initiated since; thus, the committee thought, after a long discussion, that there was no other way to avoid confusion except to ask the visitor to affirm that belief in the existence of the Grand Architect of the Universe is a basic principle of the Order.

I believe this is not too excessive and that this does not subject a foreign Brother to too harsh a test. It can no doubt be easily applied and it seems to me to be almost the minimum of what we should require. Consider, my Brethren, that it is not sufficient to not deny the existence of the Grand Architect of the Universe. It is a basic principle of the Order and we have the right to ask that this belief be affirmed. We would have been exempt from this duty if the ill-advised act by the Grand Orient of France had not raised the issue. If a schism results, the responsibility will fall on those who created it. Our only interest is to protect the ancient rules of the Order, and we should ensure that they leave our hands as we received them.

It therefore seems to me that it is impossible for us to remain silent, and as painful as it is for us to act in opposition to another large Masonic authority from a foreign country, I maintain that the Grand Lodge must have courage in its unquestionable opinion, that it should not hesitate to declare what it believes to be not only a truth, but a fundamental truth that forms the true base of Freemasonry, which we have professed in all the Lodges throughout the country, from generation to generation.

We reject, once and for all, that we have any intention to involve ourselves in the internal affairs of a foreign power, and declare that we are ready to welcome our foreign Brethren in the same Masonic spirit as in the past, but we also have to declare, loudly and unequivocally, that nothing will ever cause us to violate or mutilate a basic principle of the Order.

Caubet then concluded his article thus:

The Grand Lodge of England, far from being faithful to tradition, has just seriously betrayed it. It was intolerant and sectarian; it demonstrated regression and seriously compromised the interests and consideration of Masonry. We do not profess blind and absolute respect for tradition. As determined partisans of progress, we easily allow traditional ideas and customs to yield to more complete teachings and more rational customs; [...] In summary, the Grand Lodge of England has just very seriously undermined Masonry's cosmopolitan and universal spirit. It has divided our grand family into two parts: one that accepts the absolute liberty of conscience, and one that subordinates liberty to faith. [...] Masonry has diverged from its path, and we seek to bring it back.

Anthology VII

In 1877, at the time when the invocation of the GAOTU was made optional by the Convent (after reinforcement by deists only in 1849), a delegation was immediately sent to London to try to explain that in fact what was adopted was not exactly what had been adopted.

Alain BAUER[64]

Seven years later, the Grand Orient will attempt to renew relations with England.

---

[64] Bauer, *De la Régularité maçonnique*, 17. This delegation existed only in the mind of the author.

THE LETTER BY THE PRESIDENT OF THE COUNCIL OF THE ORDER[65]

Paris, November 28, 1884.

TO HIS ROYAL HIGHNESS

BRO. EDWARD-ALBERT, PRINCE OF WALES

Grand-Master of the Grand Lodge of England, etc, etc.

Very Illustrious Grand-Master,

For several years and, more particularly following the change made in 1877 to the first article of our Constitution by the General Assembly of the Grand-Orient, French Masons have been subjected to a regrettable situation by the Lodges under the jurisdiction of the Grand Lodge of England.

Our Brethren from the Grand-Orient of France have been refused entry into English lodges, even though English Masons have without exception been fraternally received in all the Lodges of the Grand-Orient of France.

The ostracism affecting French Masons can only be explained by a deplorable misunderstanding that needs to be stopped in the interest of universal Masonry.

It is with this intention, Very Illustrious Grand Master, that we believe we need to submit the following observations to you:

The Grand Lodge of England seems to believe that the Grand Orient of France, in revising the terms of an article of its Constitution, had sought to profess atheism and materialism. This interpretation of the vote taken by the General Assembly of 1877 is completely inaccurate. Indeed, the day after the vote an official circular addressed to all of the Grand-Orient's representatives to Masonic powers said the following: "Nothing has changed in the principles or practices of Masonry. French Freemasonry continues to be what it has always been, a fraternal and tolerant association. Out of respect for the

---

[65] The following three documents are reproduced in Juvanon 1926, *Vers la lumière*, 65–72.

religious and politic faith of its followers, it leaves to each, with regard to these delicate questions, the liberty of his conscience. In working toward the moral and intellectual perfecting of men and their well-being, it only asks that those who seek to be admitted have feelings of honesty and love for what is good, which will enable them to cooperate in a beneficial way in its work of progress and civilization."

Alongside this declaration, issued by the Illustrious Brother de Saint-Jean, then Chairman of the Council of the Grand-Orient of France, it is suitable to quote the final considerations on the report presented to the General Assembly of 1877, concerning the change to article 1 of our Constitution, by Brother Desmons, minister of the Reformed Church, rapporteur of the Special Committee appointed by the Convent to examine the issue, a committee that also included another Protestant minister: "May Masonry remain what it should be, that is, an institution open to all forms of progress, all moral and elevated ideas, all broad and liberal aspirations; may it never descend into the ardent arena of theological discussions which have only ever, believe the present speaker, led to trouble and persecution; may it protect itself from wanting to become a church, council, or synod, for all churches, councils, and synods have been violent and seek to persecute because they have sought to take dogma as a basis which, by nature, is essentially inquisitive and intolerant. May Masonry majestically rise above any question of church and sect; may it overshadow from its height all discussions; may it remain the broad shelter forever open to all generous and courageous minds, to all conscientious and disinterested seekers of truth, and finally to all victims of despotism and intolerance."

Such are, Very Illustrious Grand Master, the lofty considerations that led our General Assembly of 1877 to remove from our Constitution a paragraph that had only been added a few years earlier, in 1849.

The true sense and real motives for this change are today perfectly understood by the Masonic Powers which, at first, had incorrectly interpreted the vote at issue; and relations, momentarily interrupted with a few of these Powers, have today been renewed and are as cordial as ever.

Among these Powers we would mention the Supreme Council of the ancient and accepted Scottish Rite for France, whose Grand Master, Bro. Proal, attended the closing banquet of our General Assembly last September, where he gave a remarkable speech, filled with the expression of very close solidarity. Our official relations with this Supreme Council are ensured by the mutual exchange of Representatives; and, while preserving their own methods and ways of thinking, the two bodies are nonetheless working towards, in a shared and fraternal accord, the popularization of liberal and humanitarian ideals, which universal Masonry has strongly initiated.

Please allow us to hope, Very Illustrious Grand Master, that, recognizing the error spread by a few ill-informed or over-zealous Masonic publicists concerning the change made in 1877 to the text of our Constitution, you would seek to end this state of affairs that has been detrimental to our Grand family and especially to the Masons of the Grand-Orient of France whom we are duty-bound to protect and defend.

It is under the authority of this essential duty that the Grand Orient of France addresses you Great Wisdom with the hope that once enlightened by the preceding explanations and at your suggestion, the Grand Lodge of England will respond favorably, within a short time, to the pressing appeal we have the pleasure to address to you in the name and interest of universal Freemasonry.

Please accept, Very Illustrious Grand Master, our most fraternal regards.

For the Council of the Order of the Grand-Orient of France.

The President
signed: COUSIN, 33$^{\circ\circ}$,
Sov∴ Gr∴ Comm∴ Gr∴ M∴ of the Supreme Council

THE RESPONSE BY THE UNITED GRAND LODGE OF ENGLAND

UNITED GRAND LODGE OF ENGLAND

FREEMASON'S HALL, GREAT QUEEN STREET, LONDON WC

January 12, 1885

TO THE ILLUSTRIOUS BROTHER CHARLES COUSIN,

President of the Council of the Grand-Orient

Illustrious Sir and Brother,

I have been charged by the Prince of Wales, Grand Master of the United Grand Lodge of England, to acknowledge reception of your letter of November 28 of last year, concerning the current relations existing between the G.-Orient of France and the United Grand Lodge of England, and to make you aware that His Royal Highness has examined the communication of your Grand Orient concerning this important subject, with the sincere hope of learning that this distinguished Masonic body had re-established in its Constitution the ancient and essential motto of the Order, the elimination of which in 1877 led to the painful breaking off of fraternal relations between the Grand-Orient of France and the Grand Lodge of England.

The opinion expressed by the Grand-Orient that "the Grand Lodge of England seems to believe that the Grand-Orient of France, in revising the terms of an article of its Constitution, sought to profess atheism and materialism, an interpretation that is absolutely inaccurate concerning the Assembly's vote of 1877," is an opinion, I have the responsibility of declaring to you, that is based on a completely erroneous supposition.

The Grand Lodge of England never supposed that the Grand-Orient was seeking to make a formal profession of atheism or materialism; but the Grand Lodge of England maintains and has always maintained that belief in God is the first major sign of any true and authentic Masonry, and that without this belief professed as the essential principle for its existence, no association has the right to claim heritage to the traditions and practices of ancient and pure Masonry.

The abandonment of this *Landmark* (motto), in the opinion of the Grand Lodge of England, removes the key stone of the entire Masonic structure; and this is why it viewed with sincere regret the fact that the Grand-Orient of France erased from its Constitution, through the change made in 1877, the affirmation of the existence of God, and why it arrived at the conclusion, regrettably but unanimously, that fraternal relations, which had so happily existed between the two Masonic Powers, could no longer continue.

The principle that the Grand Lodge of England has so strongly maintained seems still to be denied by the Grand-Orient of France; but the Grand Lodge would be very satisfied to see this ancient *Landmark* (motto) re-inserted into the Constitution of the Grand Orient and would then be able to renew cordial and fraternal relations.

In the current situation, His Royal Highness is of the opinion that "as Grand Master of the United Grand Lodge of England, he cannot ask it to revoke its former decision and thus be associated with the destruction of the principle that the Grand Lodge and Freemasons of England have, for time immemorial, considered as the first and essential condition for their Masonic existence."

I have the honor of being, Illustrious Sir and Brother, your faithful servant and Bro.

SHADWELL H. CLERKE, Colonel,
Grand Secret. of England.

THE MEETING OF THE COUNCIL OF THE ORDER JANUARY 26, 1885

Following the last Convent, the Council of the Order thought it necessary to fraternally approach the United Grand Lodge of England, to induce this power to abolish the decision according to which, in 1878, it forbade the lodges within its jurisdiction to receive Freemasons from our federation.

This decision, as you know, was made after the vote from our General Assembly during its session of 1877, a vote that eliminated from our constitution the affirmation of the existence of God as a basic principle of the Masonic association. The measure of exclusion was motivated by a report presented to the United Grand Lodge, and which was accepted without debate, in which it said: 'Concerning the belief in the existence of the Grand Architect of the Universe as one of the principles upon which Freemasonry is founded, we cannot overlook the express negation of the principle, and we cannot recognize those who deny it.'

Such an assertion misrepresented the sense of our Convent's 1877 vote, which had nothing related to a negation, and which sought simply to assure each one of us of the absolute liberty of belief. The United Grand Lodge would not have doubted this if it had taken the trouble to read the report by our Bro. Desmons, representative of the Assembly committee, and to take note of the text of the resolution itself, which stated: 'The Assembly, considering that Freemasonry is not a religion, that it does therefore not need to affirm doctrines and dogmas in its constitution, accepts resolution n° IX.'

It was after this resolution that the Assembly accepted the following declaration, to be inserted in the fundamental pact: "It [Freemasonry] has as its principles the absolute liberty of conscience and human solidarity. It excludes no one for his beliefs."

During its 1884 session, our General Assembly, because it needed to revise its constitution, accepted a text thus written: "It [Freemasonry] has as its principles mutual tolerance, the respect of others and oneself, and the absolute liberty of conscience. Considering metaphysical conceptions to be the exclusive domain of its members' individual judgment, it refuses to make any dogmatic assertions."

Such declarations leave no pretext for the charge directed by the United Grand Lodge of England in 1878 against the Grand-Orient of France, and which we believed stemmed from a misunderstanding. It seemed to us that the passage of time should have disposed our Brethren of the United Grand Lodge toward putting an end to the state of affairs which, surely, they have not enjoyed. It was also agreeable to offer them the opportunity to finally establish, with the Grand Orient of France, official and amicable relations, which the United Grand Lodge has always rejected, well before being able to use the 1877 vote as an excuse. It is for this reason, in executing a decision made by the Council of the Order, its President sent the V. Ill. Gr. M. of the United Grand Lodge of England the complaint copied below.

The response to this opening came in the form of the complaint in the second document below, translated from the original English.

We would draw the attention of all our Brethren to these two documents. They will find in one, the doctrine of free enquiry in plain language and unrestricted tolerance; in the other, the requirement to believe, or the phrasing of a belief imposed by the collective and suffered by the individual.

Universal Freemasonry will appreciate.

IV

INTERNATIONAL RELATIONS IN THE TWENTIETH CENTURY

Brother Patmore suggests [...] that the relationship between the United Grand Lodge of England and those established in other parts of the world (both recognized and unrecognized) be explored, examined and published. [...] It would be a monumental task and one that might not lend itself to approval by the Board of General Purposes in that much confidential data just could not be revealed.

George Draffen,
"Some Aspects of International Masonic Law and Customs"
AQC 88 (1976): 92.

It is here out of question to review the whole of international Masonic relations throughout the twentieth century.[66] We would only recall:

-   the circumstances in which the Independent and Regular National Grand Lodge for France and the French Colonies (GLNI&R) was recognized by the United Grand Lodge of England on December 3, 1913,

-   the various versions of the two texts it officially published, *Aims and Relationships of the Craft* on August 5, 1920, June 20, 1938, and September 7, 1949, and the *Basic Principles for Grand Lodge Recognition* on September 4, 1929,

-   the various assessments on the issue of whether the fact of receiving the 4th degree of the Ancient and Accepted Scottish Rite automatically conferred regularity upon a Freemason,

-   and the distinction between the notion of regularity and that of recognition, recalled in 1983 by Sir James Stubbs.

---

[66] See James Daniel, "UGLE's External Relations 1950–2000: Policy and Practice", *AQC* 117 (2003): 1-47.

CREATION OF THE GLNI&R
ITS RECOGNITION BY ENGLAND[67]

In 1980, Alec Mellor took the risk of publishing what he called "the dossier of 1913",[68] eighteen letters of which seven were reproduced as facsimiles, written between September 17 and November 27, 1913. Some were found in the archives of the United Grand Lodge of England, which gave him permission to consult and publish them. In 2011, I myself was able to consult them in London where they are found in a dossier with the call number HC 25 entitled: *"Folder contains bundle of letters from Lord Ampthill, Pro. G. Master to Sir Edward Letchworth, G. Secretary [of the Grand Lodge of England]. Letters are in French and English and are typed and handwritten"*. I compared document XIII reproduced by Mellor, a letter sent by Ribaucourt to H. R. H. the Duke of Connaught, which in Mellor's book, has below the header the following date:

November
~~October~~ 8, 1913

Above this letter reproduced in facsimile, Mellor inserted the following remark: Creation of the GLNI&R

---

[67] See Alain Bernheim, "Recognition of a New Grand Lodge in France (1913)," *The Square* (December 2012): 32–35, accessed at http://www.thesquaremagazine.com/id-recognition-of-a-new-grand-lodge.html.

[68] Alec Mellor, *La Grande Loge Nationale Française* (Paris: Belfond, 1980), 245 *ff.*

With this historic letter, the new French obedience is officially soliciting its recognition; the date of October 8, 1913, which appears at the end of the letter is a mistake. It was corrected to read "November 8, 1913" on page 1.

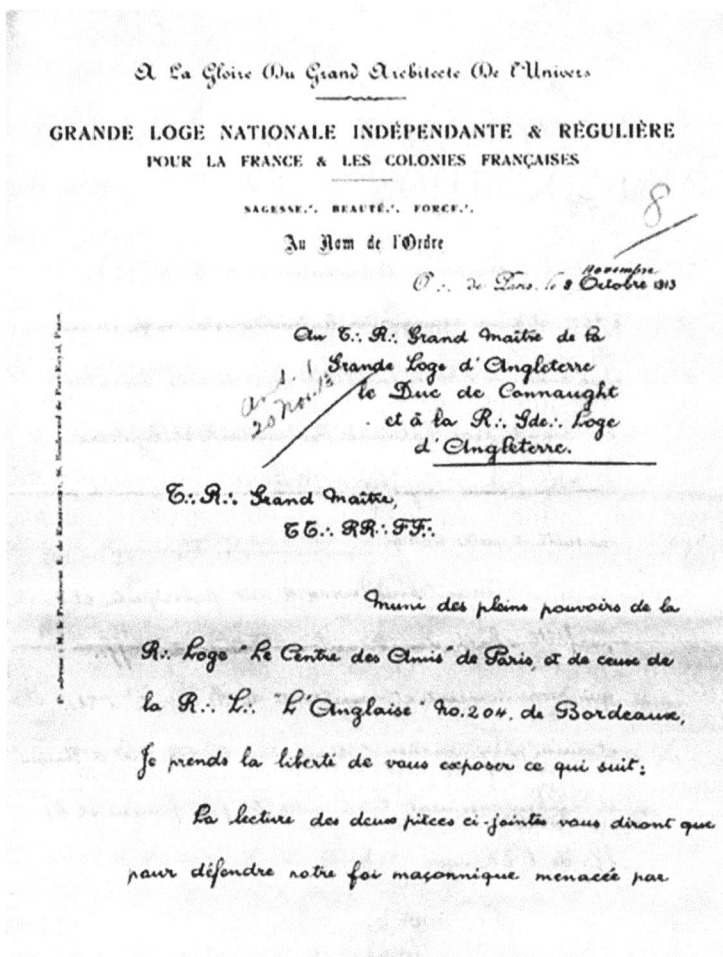

The original document

Yet on the original which I saw in London and which I have reproduced above, the word October is not crossed out as in the facsimile reproduced by Mellor and there is no date at the end of the letter.

XIII

À La Gloire Du Grand Architecte De l'Univers

GRANDE LOGE NATIONALE INDÉPENDANTE & RÉGULIÈRE
POUR LA FRANCE & LES COLONIES FRANÇAISES

SAGESSE.'. BEAUTÉ.'. FORCE.'.

Au Nom de l'Ordre

O.'. de Paris, le 8 Octobre / Novembre 1913

Au T.'. R.'. Grand Maître de la
Grande Loge d'Angleterre
le Duc de Connaught
- et à la R.'. Gde. Loge
d'Angleterre.

20 nov.

T.'. R.'. Grand Maître,
T T.'. R R.'. F F.'.

Muni des pleins pouvoirs de la
R.'. Loge "Le Centre des Amis" de Paris, et de ceux de
la R.'. L.'. "L'Anglaise" No. 204, de Bordeaux,
je prends la liberté de vous exposer ce qui suit :

La lecture des deux pièces ci-jointes vous diront que
pour défendre notre foi maçonnique menacée par

The document reproduced by Alec Mellor (page 269)

It seems in fact to be a deliberate falsification, without it being possible to establish who did it. This assumption is strengthened by a letter sent by Lord Ampthill to Ribaucourt, a letter that Mellor did not recopy with the other eighteen, but that he transcribed on pages 86–87. It says:

> We were all prepared to receive your Complaint of October 8 and you can already be fully assured that it will be welcomed.

Why was the date of October 8 'corrected' to November 8? It seems that it was because in it Ribaucourt affirmed being "Provided with the full authority of the R. Lodge 'Le Centre des Amis' of Paris, and of those of the R. L. 'L'Anglaise' No. 204 of Bordeaux." However it was only on October 29 that *L'Anglaise* wrote to Ribaucourt: "we heartily join the action of the R. L. 'Le Centre des Amis.' [...]. For the reasons you are aware of, we wish *the Grand Lodge of England to keep strictly confidential* the name of our Lodge until *further* notice. From this point, you may consider us as an entity faithful to the 'Regular and Independent National Grand Lodge,'" a letter reproduced by Mellor, pages [259–260]. The reasons mentioned by *L'Anglaise* were simple: it still belonged to the Grand Orient of France, and did not tender its resignation until December 3.[69]

December 3 was the date on which, during a meeting of the United Grand Lodge of England, Sir Edward Letchworth read a message from the Grand Master, the Duke of Connaught, officially announcing the recognition of the new French obedience:

> A body of Freemasons in France, confronted by a positive prohibition on the part of the Grand Orient to work in the name of the Great Architect of the Universe have, in fidelity to their Masonic pledges, resolved to uphold the true principles and tenets of the Craft, and have united several lodges as the Independent and Regular National Grand Lodge of France and of the French Colonies. [...] I have joyfully assented to the establishment of fraternal relations and the exchange of representatives.

During the same meeting, Lord Ampthill declared:

> The obligations which will be imposed on all Lodges under this new Constitution are the following:
>
> While the Lodge is at work the Bible will always be open on the altar.

---

[69] See the history of *L'Anglaise* on the web (http://www.anglaise204.org/page44.html) as well as the typewritten one written in 1915 by Brother Renou that I discovered in the archives of the United Grand Lodge of England (ref. 4FR 166 (204) REN), 30–32. Renou writes that the lodge was closed for the last time "in the name and under the auspices of the Grand Orient of France" on December 3, 1913.

The ceremonies will be conducted in strict conformity with the Ritual of the "Regime Rectifié" which is followed by these Lodges, a Ritual which was drawn up in 1778 and sanctioned in 1782, and with which the Duke of Kent was initiated in 1792[70].

The Lodge will always be opened and closed with invocation and in the name of the Great Architect of the Universe. All the summonses of the Order and of the Lodges will be printed with the symbols of the Great Architect of the Universe.

No religious or political discussion will be permitted in the Lodge.

The Lodge as such will never take part officially in any political affair but every individual Brother will preserve complete liberty of opinion and action.

Only those Brethren who are recognised as true Brethren by the Grand Lodge of England will be received in Lodge.

These obligations repeated word for word the text of two letters sent by Ribaucourt to London. [71]

In the letters recopied by Mellor, Ribaucourt affirmed that his new Grand Lodge would include three lodges (September 20), at least five lodges (October 23), and that "many lodges will follow us" (November 10). However, the *Anglaise 204* only joined the new French Grand Lodge the next day, December 4, which is confirmed by the text of Decree No. 2 which it received later. The third lodge of the new obedience was not dedicated until June 20, 1914.[72]

---

[70] Edward Augustus Hanover (2 November 1767-23 January 1820) was created 1st Duke of Kent on 24 April 1799 (http://www.thepeerage.com/p10078.htm#i100780). HRH was initiated on 5 August 1789 (not 'in 1790', as stated pp. 120 & 235 of *Grand Lodge 1717-1767*) in the Geneva lodge *L'Union* (not *L'Union des Cœurs*, as stated *ibid.*, p. 275). *L'Union* and *L'Union des Cœurs* were two distinct Geneva lodges. *L'Union*, founded on 20 March 1786, was the lodge of the Grand Master of the *Grand Orient National de Genève*, Jean Rodolphe Sigismond Vernet, and never worked the Rectified Rite. *L'Union des Cœurs*, founded in 1769, joined the *Régime Rectifié* in 1810 (Alain Bernheim, *Les Débuts de la Franc-Maçonnerie à Genève et en Suisse - Avec un Essai de Répertoire et de Généalogie des Loges de Genève (1736-1994)*. Genève-Paris: Champion-Slatkine. 1994, pp. 303 & 539). The dates 1778 and 1782 are those of *Convents* held in Lyon and in Wilhemsbad. The mistake concerning the lodge in which the future Duke of Kent was initiated, originated in three Swiss historians, Galiffe, Zschokke and Boos; it was set right by François Ruchon in 1935, quoted by Paul Tunbridge (*AQC* 78, 1965, p. 19). *See* Bernheim 1994 op.cit., 247 note 13 & 303 note 27.

[71] "Here are the commitments we can make," letter to Roehrich dated September 17, 1913; "We have imposed or we will impose the following obligations on our Lodges," letter to the duke of Connaught, October November 8, 1913 (facsimiles in Mellor, *La Grande Loge Nationale Française* (Paris: Belfond 1980), 247-248 and 269-[273]).

[72] Anon [=Jean Baylot], *Histoire de la Grande Loge Nationale Française 1913-1963* (Paris:

AIMS AND RELATIONSHIPS OF THE CRAFT

The first version of a document with this title is little known. Worts only quoted three lines from it.[73] It was a letter dated August 5, 1920 and signed by the Grand Secretary Colville Smith, which began as follows:

> The M. W. Grand Master has deemed it desirable, in view of attacks which have been made upon the Craft, to authorize the Grand Secretary to issue a statement defining the aims and relationships of English Freemasonry.

George Draffen republished the entire text while commenting on an article by Will Read concerning Sir Alfred Robbins,[74] President of the Board of General Purposes from 1913 to his death in 1931, which is the reason why he was nicknamed the Prime Minister of Freemasonry. Draffen recalled that the first agreement between the three British Grand Lodges was signed in 1906.

In his response, Read indicated that a conference in which the Grand Masters and Grand Secretaries of these three Grand Lodges participated, was held in Edinburgh on November 7, 1919. They declared that their alliance was essential for the defense of Masonic Landmarks, and their first, seven-point agreement anticipated that in the future none of the three Grand Lodges would enter into relations or recognize a Masonic body

---

Société parisienne d'imprimerie, 1963), 28–29, 37, 89.
[73] Worts, op. cit., 19.
[74] Will Read, "Sir Alfred Robbins," *AQC* 86 (1973): 100–135. Comments by Draffen, 129–130.

or claim this without first informing the other two and having them agree.

Read also noted that this letter dated August 5, 1920, was not in any way related to the agreement of November 1919 and that it represented a response to attacks appearing in the *Morning Post* involving only English Freemasonry.

On August 17, 1938, the Board of General Purposes presented a report to the United Grand Lodge of England[75]:

> Owing to representations which have been received with reference to the present politician situation on the Continent, and its effect upon Freemasonry, the M.W. Grand Master felt that it was desirable to obtain the opinions of the Grand Lodges of Ireland and Scotland upon the necessity for a restatement of the attitude of Freemasonry towards-political affairs and of the principles which govern our Grand Lodges in recognition of other Grand Lodges.
>
> A Conference was held in London on the 20th June last, which was attended by responsible officers of the three Home Grand Lodges. As a result of this meeting, a Statement (which is printed as an Appendix to this report) was agreed and recommended to be issued.
>
> The Board, having adopted the recommendation, is now informed that the M.W. Grand Master has authorized the Grand Secretary to issue the Statement for the information of the Craft and to take the necessary steps to ensure that the position of the Grand Lodge with respect to these matters may be fully understood.

The Freemason published the text above on September 3, 1938, followed by the text of *Aims and Relationship of the Craft*, which is in the Appendix together with the three paragraphs added in 1949 in the situation reported by Sir James Stubbs:

> The principal items of discussion were God and Communism: predominantly the latter as it was mainly a matter of trying to restrain our American Brethren from charging bull headed at the Iron Curtain, seeking to make pronouncements, which should have been self evident truths and not calling for publicity about the incompatibility of Freemasonry and Communism. In this, we were, I believe, successful, as a few paragraphs were quietly added to the 1939 *Aims and Relationships of the Craft* and quite quickly these were accepted as an integral part of the original document. When McCarthyism

---

75 Michel Brodsky, "The Regular Freemason," *AQC* 106 (1994): 114.

was finally discredited in the USA and throughout the world we heard much less of the need for every genuine Mason to fight Communism.[76]

---

[76] Sir James Stubbs, *Freemasonry in my Life* (London: Lewis Masonic, 1985), 63. The author (1910–2000), KCVO, was Grand Secretary of the United Grand Lodge of England from 1958 to 1980 then Grand Chancellor of the Supreme Council fror England and Wales from 1986 to 1994. He was also Master of *Quatuor Coronati* Lodge No. 2076 in 1968–1969.

BASIC PRINCIPLES FOR GRAND LODGE RECOGNITION

These basic principles were adopted by the United Grand Lodge of England on September 4, 1929. Will Read indicates that they were formed due to trips abroad by Sir Alfred Robbins who took note of the differences in the evaluations made by the Grand Lodges he visited. When they were adopted, Sir Alfred declared:

> The forming of such a Statement was a matter of considerable difficulty and delicacy and we were perfectly aware of the dangers attending every attempt at exact definition; but while we are not professing to satisfy every probable critic or meet every possible objection, we are well content to know that we have at length crystallised, and crystallised very clearly, these fundamental principles which have been held by English Freemasonry from the very beginning and by the Grand Lodge from its earliest assembling more than two hundred years ago.[77]

One point needs to be emphasized. While the eight principles contained in this document are generally well known—they can be found in the Appendix—, the brief introduction that precedes them is less familiar. Its last sentence is quite remarkable:

> The Board [of General Principles] desires that not only such bodies but also Brethren generally throughout the Grand Master's Jurisdiction shall be fully informed as to those Basic Principles of Freemasonry for which the Grand Lodge of England has stood throughout its history.

Indeed, while I was the first in 1988 to affirm that one single lodge (*Le Centre des Amis*) made up the GLNI&R,[78] it was then

---

[77] Quoted by Read, "Sir Alfred Robbins," *AQC* 86 (1973): 114.
[78] Alain Bernheim, "Notes on Early Freemasonry in Bordeaux (1732–1769)," *AQC* 101

generally accepted that *L'Anglaise N° 204* had taken part in its creation. The fact that the new Grand Lodge was immediately recognized even though it had only been founded by two lodges, and in spite of the fact that the first of the *Basic Principles* required at least three, was explained by the fact that its creation took place in 1913 and that the *Basic Principles* were only published sixteen years later. This was the justification made by the eminent specialist of international questions, George Draffen.[79] Yet in re-reading the introduction I have just quoted, it should be noted that it contains the claim that "these Basic Principles [*were those*] for which the Grand Lodge of England has stood throughout its history".

(1989): 98.

[79] George Draffen, "Some Aspects of International Masonic Law and Customs," *AQC* 88 (1975): 85.

DOES BELONGING TO THE A. A. S. R. AUTOMATICALLY CONFER REGULARITY?

Posed in this way, the question may cause today's readers to smile. And yet... here is what Charles Riandey,[80] then Grand Commander of the Supreme Council of France, wrote on July 22, 1964:

> Two points are established fact in Supreme Council Conferences. They are: a) that in elevating a Brother to the 4th degree, who may even be irregular as Master, he is thus conferred Scottish "regularity"; b) that the regularity of the Supreme Councils is independent from that of Grand Lodges (see Lima Conference 1958).[81]

In 1965, Yves Marsaudon wrote in a similar vein:

> [...] by the very fact of your belonging to a Lodge of Perfection working under the high authority of the Supreme Council of France, you will become a fully regular Mason. You must know, indeed, that regardless of the Obedience from which Master Masons come, their accession to the 4th degree of the Scottish Rite confers upon them absolute regularity, regularity recognized by all of the Supreme Councils of the World.[82]

But once he became Grand Commander of the Supreme Council for France, Riandey greatly changed his opinion:

> Now, one of the fundamental rules of the Ancient and Accepted Scottish Rite is that the members of the Rite's high degrees—and all the more the active members of a Supreme Council—must belong to a regular Blue Obedience. This rule is such that the presence on a Supreme Council of a single member

---

[80] See Charles Riandey's Masonic career in Bernheim, *Le rite en 33 grades*, 25–28.

[81] Letter by Charles Riandey to Georges Chadirat, July 22, 1964, (Mattei, *Chronique d'unschisme maçonnique contemporain*, Private collection reserved for M. M., 1994), 135. Bernheim, *Le rite en 33 grades*, 92).

[82] Yves Marsaudon, *De l'Initiation maçonnique à l'Orthodoxie chrétienne* (Paris: Dervy, 1965), 216.

who is not a regular Master Mason sullies with irregularity the entire Supreme Council. Some believe that for a Supreme Council to raise an irregular Master Mason to the 4th degree confers regularity upon him. This is completely inaccurate.[83]

Until the first months of 1965, the regularity of the Supreme Council of France was never in question. It participated in all the International Conferences of the Supreme Councils in the world, from the first one in Brussels in 1907 until the eighth one in 1961 in Washington, and was the host Power in Paris in 1929.

---

[83] *Message* by Charles Riandey, March 16, 1965 (Bernheim, *Le rite en 33 grades*, 620).

REGULARITY AND RECOGNITION

James Stubbs was the Grand Secretary of the United Grand Lodge of England from 1958 to 1980. The following remarks were excerpted from comments he wrote concerning an article by Christopher Haffner:

> [...] Bro. Haffner seems to be confusing 'regularity', which is subjective and capable of several interpretations, with 'recognition', which is factual. No Grand Lodge can be forced to recognize another even-if it is prepared to agree that by whatever standards it accepts it is regular. No Grand Lodge can demand recognition; it can only ask for it and submit what it believes to be a good case. Conversely, if it so wishes a Grand Lodge can break off relations, that is, 'derecognize' another if it feels that there is good reason to do so. Several examples in our own time could be quoted and it is not always the 'senior' Grand Lodge that takes the action.
>
> I would prefer after some years of experience, and of working with such experts as Raymond Brooke (Ireland), Judge Froessel (New York) and not least Sir Ernest Cooper, to take the view that it is as important for the Grand Lodge which is being solicited to look for reasons for *not* granting recognition as for the soliciting Grand Lodge to adduce reasons for receiving it. This may seem to be a negative policy; on the other hand, while it is a counsel of perfection that no recognition should be granted to a Grand Lodge that recognizes others that we (of England) do *not* recognize — not least because recognition is a fluid matter and a list presented in 1980 may well have had additions of less desirable nature by 1983 — it must be accepted that to continue recognition of a Grand Lodge which has in its list of recognitions other bodies which are not recognized is inviting trouble and embarrassment. It does not conduce to the dignity of the senior Grand Lodge if those responsible for advising it found after a short time that a recognition needs to be rescinded.[84]

---

[84] James Stubbs, commenting Christopher Haffner's "Regularity of Origin", *AQC* 96 (1983): 132.

In other words, the remark made by Roger Dachez in 2011, "It is however indisputable that, without recognition from London, an obedience is not regular", does not match reality.

V
THE TWENTY-FIRST CENTURY

I am a French Freemason, but I do not belong to any French Masonic body as an active member. I am not qualified to participate in any way in this essential year of 2014 for French Freemasonry. But I am a historian of Freemasonry. In this regard, what I have read over the last few years by French Masons has often shocked me, not due to the opinions expressed, but due to the alleged, invented, or inaccurate historical facts upon which they were based.

It is true that the writings and deeds of English Masonry I have sought to recall as scrupulously as possible in the preceding pages may often be disconcerting. In a paper appearing this year, I indicated the blindness of our English Brethren during the years before and after the Second World War.[85]

But I also discovered the speech[86] given by Lord Northampton[87] during the *Cornerstone Society* conference in summer 2005. He began cautiously, saying in essence that what he was about to say only reflected his own ideas and were not necessarily those of the Grand Lodge of England, where he was *Pro Grand Master*.[88] After indicating that with 272,000

---

[85] Alain Bernehim, "United Grand Lodge and United Grand Lodges of Germany, 1946–1961," *AQC* 127 (2014): 61–103.

[86] http://freemasonry.bcy.ca/events/vmc_townhall2012/Cornerstone_Society_Whither_directing _our_ course_2.pdf.

[87] Spencer Douglas David Compton, 7th Marquess of Northampton. Born April 2, 1946. Deputy Grand Director of Ceremonies 1983–1985, Grand Sword Bearer 1992, Senior Grand Warden 1994–1995, Assistant Grand Master since 1995. Pro Grand Master from March 2001 to March 2008. Details concerning his secular life on *Wikipedia* (https://en.wikipedia.org/wiki/Spencer_Compton,_7th_Marquess_of_Northampton).

[88] When the Grand Master is a member of the royal family, he is able to appoint a Pro Grand Master who occupies the second highest rank in the hierarchy protocol of the United Grand

members, his Grand Lodge was by far the largest in the world in terms of numbers, he then added: "But something is wrong with Anglo Saxon Freemasonry."

He recognized that it had lost 40% of its membership over the last thirty years while the number of its lodges had increased. As a result, many of these lodges were having trouble surviving due to the small number of members. Another result is that the brothers were accepting new members without always checking to see if they had the required qualities to receive the initiation. Even worse: if, in the best of cases, the lodges were able to initiate one candidate per year, they rushed the poor man to the third degree without giving him the time to catch his breath and understand what this meant. Six years later, such candidates became Worshipful Masters or had found an excuse to resign and never return. This is not Freemasonry as it should be lived, and is hardly better than the one-day classes[89] in the United-States that we all lament.

Towards the end of his speech, he said some things that will surprise those who only have a superficial understanding of English Freemasonry:

> Let me stress that you cannot discover the mysteries of Freemasonry by reading the ritual book. You have to go through the process of initiation to realize and unlock the mystery, because it is a felt experience.[90]

One year later, again during a *Cornerstone Society* conference, Julian Rees said:

> A peculiar system of morality, veiled in allegory and illustrated by symbols. This is the answer to the question, "What is Freemasonry?" [...] This is, and is intended to be, a quick answer which endeavours to describe that which, in

---

[89] Lodge of England.
Meetings during which candidates are initiated and receive the 32nd degree over the course of two or three successive days.

[90] In October 2014, Marc Henry, Grand Master of the Grand Lodge of France, expressed the same idea: "Only then will he begin his initiation process, for we are an initiatiory Order that rets upon values of intellectual, ethical and spiritual progress that will allow him to go beyond his initial condition." Accessed at http://www.gldf.org/fr/qui-sommes-nous/articles-de-presse/1083-extrait-de-qinfo-chaloncomq-du-23-octobre-2014.

fact, cannot be described in words of one syllable, indeed may not be described adequately in words at all.

I recalled the preceding quotations in a presentation I gave in 2010 to members of the Association for Masonic Research and the Sheffield Masonic Study Circle in Manchester.[91] There I quoted Lepage:

> The Order—traditional and initiatory Freemasonry—has no historically-known origin. [...] The Obediences, on the contrary, are recent creations, of which we can—although with some difficulty and inaccuracies —describe the birth, and whose existence is then well known in most of the details.[92]

I spoke of my aversion to explaining our symbols because, as Julian Rees said, nothing that is expressed in words—instructions or conferences—makes it possible to hear Freemasonry's little night music.

I could have mentioned (I did not) words written by Alain Bauer and Édouard Boeglin in 2003, which I quoted earlier:

> The year 1865 was an occasion for a fundamental debate which only really concluded in 1877 with the disappearance of the required reference to the Grand Architect of the Universe in the constitutional texts. [...] the elimination of the Grand Architect in 1877 [...] The Grand Orient thus took leave of the Grand Architect.

And then compared them with what Corneloup[93] wrote, whose first article as the new editor of *Symbolisme* in December 1945 was titled *Plaidoyer pour le Grand Architecte de l'Univers* [*Appeal for the Grand Architect of the Universe*]. Long excerpts can be found in the appendix.

Can it then be implied that within the same obedience, diametrically opposed opinions may co-exist? Or is it rather the

---

[91] Alain Bernheim, "My Approach to Masonic History," *Transactions of the Manchester Association for Masonic Research*, Volume CII (2011): 75–90.
[92] Lepage, *L'ORDRE et les Obédiences*, 8.
[93] Initiated at the Grand Orient of France in 1908, member of the Grand College of Rites, Supreme Council, on June 16, 1945. Gran Commander from 1958 to 1962, then Honorary Grand Commander *ad vitam*. A few months after becoming a member of the Grand College of Rites, he succeeded Oswald Wirth who died in March 1943, and became editor of *Le Symbolisme*.

interpretations given to the symbols through words that are the source of these oppositions?

> Liberty of conscience allows us to view the Grand Architect of the Universe as each person sees fit, but we have no right to impose our own personal view on our Brethren.[94]

Anderson wrote the same thing twice in 1738:

> And whatever are our different Opinions in other Things (leaving all Men to Liberty of Conscience) [..]

> They [the disciples of Zoroaster] are here mention'd, and not for their Religious Rites that are not the Subject of this Book: For we leave every Brother to Liberty of Conscience; but strictly charge him carefully to maintain the Cement of the Lodge, and the 3 Articles of NOAH.[95]

---

[94] Speech by Claude Collin, Sovereign Grand Commander of the Supreme Council of France, during the Celebration of the Scottish Order, on December 15, 2013 in Paris.

[95] James Anderson, *The New Book of Constitutions* (1738), v and 23. Regarding the religious basis of the first Grand Lodge after 1717 and liberty of conscience, see Lewis Edwards, "Anderson's Book of Constitutions of 1738," *AQC* 46 (1936): 360–361.

APPENDICES

BASIC PRINCIPLES FOR GRAND LODGE RECOGNITION

Accepted by the Grand Lodge, September 4, 1929

The M. W. The Grand Master having expressed a desire that the Board would draw up a statement of the Basic Principles on which this Grand Lodge could be invited to recognize any Grand Lodge applying for recognition by the English Jurisdiction, the Board of General Purposes has gladly complied. The result, as follows, has been approved by the Grand Master, and it will form the basis of a questionnaire to be forwarded in future to each Jurisdiction requesting English recognition. The Board desire that not only such bodies but the Brethren generally throughout the Grand Master's Jurisdiction shall be fully informed as to those Basic Principles of Freemasonry for which the Grand Lodge of England has stood throughout its history.

Regularity of origin; i.e., each Grand Lodge shall have been established lawfully by a duly recognized Grand Lodge or by three or more regularly constituted Lodges.

That a belief in the G. A. O. T. U. and His revealed will shall be an essential qualification for membership.

That all Initiates shall take their Obligation on or in full view of the open Volume of the Sacred Law, by which is meant the revelation from above that is binding on the conscience of the particular individual who is being initiated.

That the membership of the Grand Lodge and individual Lodges be exclusively men; and that each Grand Lodge shall have no Masonic intercourse of any kind with mixed Lodges or bodies which admit women to membership.

That the Grand Lodge shall have sovereign jurisdiction over the Lodges under its control; i.e. that it shall be a responsible, independent, self-governing organization, with sole and undisputed authority over the Craft or Symbolic Degrees (Entered Apprentice, Fellow Craft, and Master Mason) within its Jurisdiction; and shall not in any way be subject to, or divide such authority with, a Supreme Council or other Power claiming any control or supervision over those degrees.

That the three Great Lights of Freemasonry (namely, the Volume of Sacred Law, the Square, and the Compasses) shall always be exhibited when the Grand Lodge or its subordinate Lodges are at work, the chief of these being the Volume of the Sacred Law.

That the discussion of religion and politics within the Lodge shall be strictly prohibited.

That the principles of the Antient Landmarks, customs, usages of the Craft shall be strictly observed.

Anthology VIII

It was the United Grand Lodge of England which, once for all, defined the criteria for Masonic regularity on September 4, 1929, with the desire to have them applied universally.

Cécile RÉVAUGER, 2000[96]

---

[96] Cécile Révauger, *Encyclopédie de la Franc-Maçonnerie* (Paris: La Pochotèque, 2000), under "Régularité."

BASIC PRINCIPLES (1989)

Freemasonry is practised under many independent Grand Lodges with principles or standards similar to those set by the United Grand Lodge of England throughout its history.

Standards

To be recognised as regular by the United Grand Lodge of England, a Grand Lodge must meet the following standards.

1.It must have been lawfully established by a regular Grand Lodge or by three or more private Lodges, each warranted by a regular Grand Lodge.

2.It must be truly independent and self-governing, with undisputed authority over Craft - or basic - Freemasonry (i. e. the symbolic degrees of Entered Apprentice, Fellow Craft and Master Mason) within its jurisdiction, and not subject in any other way to or sharing power with any other Masonic body.

3.Freemasons under its jurisdiction must be men, and it and its Lodges must have no Masonic contact with Lodges which admit women to membership.

4.Freemasons under its jurisdiction must believe in a Supreme Being.

5.All Freemasons under its jurisdiction must take their Obligations on or in full view of the Volume of the Sacred Law (i. e. the Bible) or the book held sacred by the man concerned.

6.The three Great Lights of Freemasonry (i. e. the Volume of the Sacred Law, the Square and the Compasses) must be on display when the Grand Lodge or its Subordinate Lodges are open.

7.The discussion of religion and politics within its Lodges must be prohibited.

8.It must adhere to the established principles and tenets (the 'Antient Landmarks') and customs of the Craft, and insist on their being observed within its Lodges.

Irregular or unrecognised Grand Lodges

There are some self-styled Masonic bodies which do not meet these standards, e. g. which do not require a belief in a Supreme Being, or which allow or encourage their members to participate as such in political matters. These bodies are not recognised by the Grand Lodge of England as being Masonically regular, and Masonic contact with them is forbidden.

January 1989

AIMS AND RELATIONSHIPS OF THE CRAFT (SEPTEMBER 3, 1938)

In August 1938 the Grand Lodges of England, Ireland and Scotland each agreed upon and issued a statement identical in terms except that the name of the issuing Grand Lodge appeared throughout. This statement, which was entitled "Aims and Relationships of the Craft," was in the following terms:

1. From time to time the United Grand Lodge of England has deemed it desirable to set forth in precise form the aims of Freemasonry as consistently practised under its jurisdiction since it came into being as an organised body in 1717, and also to define the principles governing its relations with those other Grand Lodges with which it is in fraternal accord.

2. In view of representations which have been received, and of statements recently issued which have distorted or obscured the true objects of Freemasonry, it is once again considered necessary to emphasise certain fundamental principles of the Order.

3. The first condition of admission into, and membership of, the Order is a belief in the Supreme Being. This is essential and admits of no compromise.

4. The Bible, referred to by Freemasons as the Volume of the Sacred Law, is always open in the Lodges. Every candidate is required to take his obligation on that Book, or on the Volume which is held by his particular Creed to impart sanctity to an oath or promise taken upon it.

5. Everyone who enters Freemasonry is, at the outset, strictly forbidden to countenance any act which may have a tendency to subvert the peace and good order of society, he must pay due obedience to the law of any state in which he resides or which may afford him protection, and he must never be remiss in the allegiance due to the Sovereign of his native land.

6. While English Freemasonry inculcates in each of its members the duties of loyalty and citizenship, it reserves to the individual the right to hold his own opinion with regard to public affairs. But neither in any Lodge nor at any time in his capacity as a Freemason is he permitted to discuss or to advance his views on theological or political questions.

7. The Grand Lodge has always consistently refused to express any opinion on questions of foreign or domestic state policy either at home or abroad, and it will not allow its name to be associated with an action however

humanitarian it may appear to be, which infringes its unalterable policy of standing aloof from every question affecting the relations between one Government and another, or between political parties, or questions as to rival theories of Government.

8. The Grand Lodge is aware that there do exist bodies styling themselves Freemasons, which do not adhere to these principles, and while that attitude exists the Grand Lodge refuses absolutely to have any relations with such bodies or to regard them as Freemasons.

9. The Grand Lodge of England is a sovereign and independent body practising Freemasonry only within the three Degrees and only within the limits defined in its Constitution as "pure Ancient Freemasonry." It does not recognise or admit the existence of any superior Masonic authority however styled.

10. On more than one occasion the Grand Lodge has refused, and it will continue to refuse, to participate in conferences with so-called International Associations claiming to represent Freemasonry, which admit to membership bodies failing to conform strictly to the principles upon which the Grand Lodge of England is founded. The Grand Lodge does not admit any such claim, nor can its views be represented by any such Association.

11. There is no secret with regard to any of the basic principles of Freemasonry, some of which have been stated above. The Grand Lodge will always consider the recognition of those Grand Lodges which profess and practise and can show that they have consistently professed and practised, those established and unaltered principles, but in no circumstances will it enter into discussion with a view to any new or varied interpretation of them. They must be accepted and practised wholeheartedly and in their entirety by those who desire to be recognised as Freemasons by the United Grand Lodge of England.

PARAGRAPHS ADDED AND APPROVED ON SEPTEMBER 7, 1949

The Grand Lodge of England was asked if it still maintained the terms of this declaration, paragraph 7 in particular. The Grand Lodge of England responded that it held to every word of its declaration and has since asked for the opinion of the Grand Lodges of Ireland and Scotland. A Conference was held between these three Grand Lodges and all, without hesitation, reaffirmed the Declaration made in 1939: nothing related to current events was found that would lead them to reconsider their position.

If ever Freemasonry deviated from its line, by expressing an opinion on political or theological questions, it would be called upon not only to publicly approve or denounce any movement that may arise in the future, but it would sow discord among its own members.

The three Grand Lodges are convinced that it is only by strictly adhering to this policy that Freemasonry has survived the constant changes in doctrines in the outside world and they are forced to officially declare their complete disapproval of any action that may authorize the smallest breach in the basic principles of Freemasonry. They are convinced that if one of the three Grand Lodges acted in this way, it could no longer claim to be following the Ancient Landmarks of the Order and would in the end be exposed to disintegration.

IN DEFENSE OF THE GRAND ARCHITECT OF THE UNIVERSE

J. CORNELOUP

If the study of Masonic Symbolism had not been unfortunately neglected in the nineteenth century, as people found themselves fascinated by the development of Science, which they expected would provide the key to all mysteries, the quarrel over the Grand Architect of the Universe could probably have been avoided. It was largely due to a lack of understanding, resulting from a lack of information, and under the influence of preconceived ideas that spiritualists as well as materialists confronted each other, even though they both agreed on one point: they identified the Grand Architect of the Universe with God.

The latter declare: *"Accepting this symbol means to adopt a spiritualist position which is impossible for us to accept."*

The former reply: *"Rejecting the symbol means to adhere to the atheism condemned by Anderson. We cannot subscribe to it."*

I note in passing that if intolerance has degrees, the intolerance of the intransigent supporters of the Grand Architect surpasses that of their opponents. Indeed, imposing this symbol while identifying it with God is to demand of all Masons a deist profession of faith, while it is arbitrary to believe that leaving Masons to decide whether or not to use the phrase "Grand Architect of the Universe" is tantamount to an adherence to atheism: it is simply a prudently neutral position that respects each person's liberty of conscience.

This is precisely the argument of the Grand Orient. It would be irrefutable if, as I hope to demonstrate, it did not result in an unfortunate mutilation of Masonic Symbolism which it decapitates of an essential element, thereby obscuring the deep significance of all Freemasonry; and if, on the other hand, a series of regrettable circumstances, misunderstandings, exaggerated and awkward comments sometimes made the 1877 decision seem like a victory for free-thinkers over believers, for materialists over spiritualists, it could only concern and irritate the latter who, strengthened by their predominant influence in Anglo-Saxon Freemasonry (the largest element by far in worldwide Freemasonry) responded by claiming the right of the first occupier: *"The house belongs to us; you are the ones who have to leave."*

Had they forgotten that the house had specifically been built as a place of assembly for all men of good will, regardless of philosophical and religious opinions?

Once the split was consummated between the Grand Orient and Anglo-Saxon Freemasonries the situation only became more complicated with all the incidents and interpretations it elicited in spite of some worthy efforts to bring the question back down to size.

In all countries, there are a majority of Masons for whom tolerance is not just a word but a virtue they endeavor to practice. Often lacking in historical and symbolic knowledge which would allow them to make a judgment based on the matter at issue, they allow themselves to be influenced by the sharp contentions they hear coming from their respective environments: in this way, a situation dominated by passion instead of reason perpetuates itself.

This study is intended for those who do not believe they hold the truth but are seeking it, which is more Masonic and praiseworthy. This study will not provide this truth, but arguments for them to meditate and weigh.

Let us first emphasize that it is arbitrary and improper to consider the question exclusively from a metaphysical point of view. Our first concern will be to reposition it on the proper ground: Masonic Symbolism. This symbolism is very mixed. Freemasonry inherited disparate contributions from ancient Initiations, contributions which are not all authentic. Without attempting to depreciate the high teachings handed down by the Wisdoms of Antiquity, it can be said that symbols of corporate origin are, among all, those that speak most clearly to our understanding and at the same time those that are the most complete and coherent; they are specifically Masonic, worthy, and come to us directly from operative Freemasonry, from whence comes our speculative Freemasonry.

The mallet and chisel, the rule and lever, the plumb line and level, the square and compass, the trowel and apron, all tools or accessories of the operative mason, characterize the various parts of the initiation work, even for minds that are the least prepared for esoteric speculation. Similarly, the materials, the rough stone being hewn and then transformed into a square stone, indicate in a precise way the idea of education and adaptation to social life.

With these tools and materials, the Mason must build the Temple. It is first the dark room where the apprentice focuses his attention and efforts on the inner work he must accomplish in himself; then windows are pierced, which enables the fellow to become aware of the outside world and study it; finally, once the four doors are opened facing the four cardinal points, the Master will be able to leave the Middle Chamber and travel the world from the North to the South and from the East to the West, not simply to know it, but especially to work constructively in it. All of this is full of teachings.

We have the tools; we have the materials; we have the worker. The Symbolism is however not complete. Before the tracing board, which I did not mention earlier but has not been forgotten, there is an empty spot. The one missing is the one who, in using the square, ruler, and compass, draws the plans, decides what is needed, calculates the dimensions, organizes the work, and distributes the tasks. Where then is the reason that guides, the science that calculates, the intelligence that inspires, and the art that embellishes?

Hiram?

Yes, we have Hiram. But Hiram is outside of operative Masonry which borrowed him from a dubious Hebrew legend. And Hiram, even decorated with the title of architect, is primarily an entrepreneur, a site manager, a leader of men. This is certainly a useful and even honorable role, but one that does not allow us to imagine Hiram in front of the tracingd board. In this eminent place where thought develops, we need someone greater than Hiram. We are thus led to remember that pure Masonic tradition had not given a double to Hiram, but placed over him the Grand Architect of the Universe, a logical and necessary coronation of its symbolic building.

If those who have gone before us had been content to name their symbol *"the Architect"*, and nothing more, they would have spared us a great deal of trouble. If need be, the epithet *"gran"* could even have been acceptable without arousing too strong a reaction, in light of the tendency for the founders of the Order to over-emphasize. But GRAND ARCHITECT OF THE UNIVERSE! It was too much, enough at least so that later the symbol's partisans and adversaries agreed (although for opposite reasons) in affirming that the Grand Architect is GOD and could only be GOD.

With just the Architect, we could have had at least a chance of remaining within Masonry. With the Grand Architect of the Universe, we were projected into the middle of metaphysics. Should then the term be condemned? Before judging the symbol, we should at least seek what it covers and, to guide our study, we should recall what the very foundation of Symbolism is.

[...]

We should devote ourselves to this search for the Grand Architect of the Universe.

Of course, believers in all the religions and desists have the right of identifying him to God. The error and misuse is to forbid others the freedom to search for other interpretations.

Deists will see in it the Creator of all things, which is very near, but still different.

For spiritualists, the Grand Architect will be the Supreme Intelligence, soul and driving force of the world.

For philosophers who make Humanism a religion without a god, it would be the collective conscience of Humanity.

Before going further, let us observe that between the most common conception of God and the notion of the Grand Architect, a key distinction can be made: God created the world out of nothing, or at least out of Non-Being. He is above all the Creator, through an operation that surpasses our reason and our ability to apprehend. The Grand

Architect, however, does not claim to create. He arranges in a certain order existing material: ORDO AB CHAO. He is an organizer, a builder, a role available to our understanding and which does not offend our reason.

By meditating on this and proceeding deductively, we will draw out the following interpretation: THE GRAND ARCHITECT IS THE SYMBOL OF THE LAWS AND FORCES THAT RULE OVER UNIVERSAL EVOLUTION AND ORDER THE COSMOS IN A WAY THAT IS ALWAYS MORE HARMONIOUSLY SUITABLE FOR THE CONDITIONS OF LIFE.

This interpretation does not escape the reproach of finalism, because it can be opposed by the following: *"An architect builds according to a preconceived plan. The Grand Architect thus implies a predetermined universe, which is incompatible with current scientific data!"*

I do not subscribe to this condemnation. I willingly concede that symbolic language does not always stand up to the rigorous correctness of terms. It can thus put off those who have become accustomed to the precise vocabulary of scientific studies. (We would also note that there are words invented specifically to refer to that which escapes our understanding: *"soporific virtue"* is a convenient phrase but it generates many illusions.)

I ask then that we not take the term architect in an absolutely literal sense. It was chosen by our predecessors because they were Masons. Had they been surveyors, they might have adopted the term Grand Geometrician: the symbol would have been the same, but the specious argument claiming to demonstrate the finalism of the symbol would not have held up.

The following objection is more relevant: finalism is not only the result of the word *"architect"*. It is included in the interpretation which attributes to the laws of evolution and organization of matter in the universe a role assimilable to that of a directing intelligence, even though evolution seems to have occurred in an entirely fortuitous and experimental way: all combinations possible took place during the infinity of time but the only ones to survive were those that were stable in the conditions of that moment.

[...]

∴

I know well the responses that will come: *"If we accept that the extrapolations you used are legitimate, which is debatable, it remains that you have used them in such a way that if Masonry aligned itself with your point of view, it would have to renounce agnosticism, which is its essential rule."*

Now we come to the heart of the issue. *"Freemasonry must be rigorously agnostic."* I have thought so. I have said so. I even believe to have written it. But I feel no shame in recognizing that I was wrong. No, Masonry cannot be agnostic and is not agnostic. Re-read the Constitution of the Grand Orient of France and weigh its terms: you will see that it implies at least two premises. The first is that humanity's evolution moves toward Progress; the second is that human work and reason are effective tools that contribute to this progress. We are so used to these ideas that they seem entirely natural and we no longer perceive that they imply an entire philosophy, an obvious GNOSIS. This forbids us from maintaining without contradiction that Freemasonry is or must be agnostic.

Whoever accepts a discipline only if agnosticism is the rule cannot be a Freemason without being inconsistent with himself, because he will have to subscribe to a constitution that goes against agnosticism. In fact, he has but one recourse: to dedicate himself to Science and cloister himself in a laboratory as closed to the world as the most hermetic monastery. For as soon as we enter even slightly into life, we are obliged to abandon the agnostic position. The least human experience proves that there is no practical, daily, or exceptional problem than can be resolved with the full and true knowledge of its cause: there is always something that remains unknown, and yet we must make a decision. But Freemasonry is the Art of Living. Philosophically, to be a Freemason means to want to live according to a certain rule we believe suitable to guide us not only towards TRUTH, but also towards PROGRESS and BEAUTY. It thus means to deliberately choose, from among diverse philosophical positions, the one we deem conforms best to the necessary rule. This implies a true act of faith in the progressivity of human evolution, a particular instance of universal evolution. By pushing the analysis further and generalizing, to be a Freemason is to accept that everything occurs as if the Cosmos has been bathed in some kind of force field that polarizes all the factors of evolution, directing them towards an increasingly perfect organization, tending towards an ideal of harmony.

And since Masonry is symbolically the image of the world, this is altogether perhaps what, Oswald Wirth called *"the directing spirit of Freemasonry"*. Even though understood in this way, the term directing spirit implies nothing specifically spiritualist, in order to avoid any criticism, I will substitute this term with directing principle, and conclude that for the Freemason the best interpretation of the Grand Architect is the following: *"The Grand Architect symbolizes the directing principle of Freemasonry and of the Universe"*. To work for the glory of the Grand Architect of the Universe could thus signify, *ad libitum*:

—either working under the sign of God;

—or working under the inspiration of the collective conscience of humanity;

—or working according to the directing principle that directs the evolution of the world and of humanity toward Progress.

Once this is understood and accepted, who could argue that the Grand Orient would be betraying its mission and undermining the liberty of conscience if it decided to restore the symbol of the Grand Architect of the Universe?

Without exhausting the topic, I believe I have clearly brought out the main aspects of the Grand Architect according to the specific perspectives of religions, philosophies, Science and Freemasonry.

But I said that a symbol fulfills its key function only if it creates a link between all of its followers which, aside from their particular beliefs, provides them with a mutual understanding of their points of view.

Well! For the Grand Architect, the shared idea that ties together the various interpretations is that they all incline us to conceive of a principle of progressive and harmonious organization in the world. This is why the Grand Architect is a perfect symbol. When it is missing, it lets the top of the monument of our Symbolism unfinished and bare.

I cannot emphasize this key point enough. If I have truly succeeded in expressing my thought, I hope I have made it clear how the absence of the symbol is detrimental, not only to Symbolism, but to Masonic doctrine itself.

Freemasonry honors Science as a tool that is essential for its work. But if Freemasonry were limited to Science, it would be useless and superfluous.

Like Science, Freemasonry invites us to seek for what is genuine. But beyond Science, and because he believes in Progress, the Mason also seeks for the Good. And in this dual quest, he cannot help but discover how harmonious are the laws that govern the world: he acquires at the same time a sense and desire for Beauty.

I have one final argument to discuss. The least scientific, but the most human, therefore one that in fact weighs most heavily on most people's minds: *"We refuse to go to Canossa!"*

What I have already said demonstrates sufficiently, I believe, that the Grand Architect is compatible with any philosophy that accepts progress. Its recognition can thus not be interpreted as an abdication of the doctrines dear to us. It would thus be false and slanderous to claim that the Grand Orient would go to Canossa if it began again to use a symbol shared with the rest of Freemasonry. Such a decision would be justified in every way. It is particularly timely at a moment when strengthening ties with universal Freemasonry could have considerable positive repercussions.[97]

As for myself, I am even more sensitive than those who are afraid to go to Canossa. Even though I know I'm not headed there, I do not want to give dishonest critics of the Grand Orient the opportunity to insinuate that, just as Paris was worth a mass, recognition by the Anglo-Saxons could be worth kneeling down before the Grand Architect. This would surely be said or whispered if we were waiting for the decision to be asked of us (people would quickly say: *demanded*) from the outside.

My conclusion is thus that the Grand Orient would make itself greater and command everyone's respect, even the ill-intentioned, if it adopted this restorative measure at its own initiative, before the issue is raised by others.

---

[97] [Note added in the reprint of this article in 1965:] I recall that this article was written in 1945. The "strengthening" I mentioned failed. This is not a reason to despair.

N° 245   Revue Mensuelle   Décembre 1945

LE SYMBOLISME

ORGANE D'INITIATION
A LA PHILOSOPHIE DU GRAND ART
DE LA
CONSTRUCTION UNIVERSELLE

Directeur-Fondateur :
Oswald WIRTH (1912-1943)

SOMMAIRE :

DIRECTION ET ADMINISTRATION :
« Le Symbolisme », 68, rue Marjolin, Levallois-Perret (Seine)

RÉDACTEUR EN CHEF :
Marius LEPAGE, 9, rue de la Cointerie, Laval (Mayenne)

'AN INTERVIEW WITH ALAIN BERNHEIM'

MIKE KEARSLEY
EDITOR OF *THE SQUARE,*
THE INDEPENDENT MAGAZINE FOR FREEMASONS
SEPTEMBER 2015

1. Tell us a little about your background, your career and how you became involved in Freemasonry

As a French citizen I became a Mason of the Grand Orient de France – that 'irregular body' –, in 1963, then in 1973 of the Grande Loge Nationale Française – a regular one. Later in 1977, a member of the United Grand Lodges of Germany and, for the past twenty-four years, of the Swiss Grand Lodge Alpina.

In the 1960s, I lived in a small German town and gave about one hundred (piano) concerts each year. One day, I was asked if I was interested in Freemasonry. I knew next to nothing about Freemasonry at that time. There were two lodges belonging to the Grand Orient of France in Germany, one of them near to the French border in Saarbrücken. I was made there in 1963. Two German lodges existed in the same town but they never visited us and we never visited them. I asked why and was told it was a complicated matter, which I would understand later.

2. How and why did you become involved in Masonic research?

At that time all I knew about Freemasonry came from a book by Roger Peyrefitte, *Les Fils de la Lumière*. It was rather well-informed and included an interesting portrait of a member of the Grand Orient,

Marius Lepage. Lepage was Worshipful Master of a small lodge in Normandy as well as the Editor of an excellent quarterly Masonic review, *Le Symbolisme*. He had written a book which came into my hands, *L'ORDRE et les Obédiences*.

Not being familiar with German, Lepage did not mention a single book written in that language and probably never suspected that the earliest reliable history of French Freemasonry was written in German in the middle of the nineteenth century by Dr. Georg Kloss. He underlined the importance of the English authentic school, of books by Knoop, Jones and Hamer, and of *Ars Quatuor Coronatorum*. I got the catalogue from Marks & Co. in Charing Cross Road and bought my first original Gould in red morocco for £2- 15 shillings.

As soon as I was a Master Mason, I applied to become a member of *Quatuor Coronati* Corresponding Circle. My application was accepted and I subscribed for advance copies of papers. I bought everything there was to buy.

Soon afterwards, I sent a few pages of comments on Eric Ward's paper, 'Anderson's Freemasonry not Deistic'. Ward gave his interpretation of Anderson's First Charge and I thought fit to summarize the views of two respected continental Brethren, J. Corneloup and Bernhard Beyer. Bro. Carr accepted my comments except for one sentence of Corneloup which he crossed out:

And since I am myself an atheist, and because I know other atheists (very few in numbers, for genuine atheists are very rare) who belong to the best Freemasons, I have the right to state that all of them have a religious and a moral sense at least equal to that of the average Christian, of the average Jew, of the average Muslim, and no one thinks for one second to forbid them admittance into our Temples.

Carr had written in the margin:

To boast being an atheist and having a religious sense is playing upon words and trying to confuse issues.

To which I replied:

This is not only the problem of Corneloup, of Bernheim, of Carr... It is the problem of words [...] For most of us it is not possible to be an atheist and have a religious sense. Corneloup says it is possible for him. [....] who is going to decide if Corneloup is right or wrong ?

In the mean time, having merely followed references given by Kloss and Gould, I had unearthed two essential documents considered as lost forever: the French Grand Lodge General Regulations of 1743 and the Statutes of St John of Jerusalem of 1755. I announced my discovery in 1967 during a conference in Paris on the History of Freemasonry. As a consequence, I became a member of the History Committee of the Grand Orient of France.

However in January 1970 I got an unexpected letter from Carr:

We have received information that although you are apparently attached to perfectly respectable lodges in Germany, you are also a member of the French Grand Orient. If this is true, we would not be able to keep you upon our Roll of Members and I must ask you to let me have a declaration certified by the Secretary of your Lodge and stating that you are not in any way involved with that irregular and unrecognized body. I shall hope to hear from you at your early convenience. Yours sincerely and fraternally.

I answered immediately, explaining the limited information (the name and location of your lodge, but not the Grand Lodge it belongs to) asked from the registration file I had sent to London and that in my Grand Orient Lodge I belonged to at that time in Strasbourg the Three Great Lights were displayed and that our ritual was always open and closed in the name of the G.A.O.T.U. Carr's reply was very friendly:

I am deeply sorry to have lost a friend and fellow-student whom I valued highly. [...] we will gladly re-instate you (without fee) upon your resignation from the Grand Orient, and your application from a regular and recognized Lodge.

I realized that my membership in the Grand Orient was a mistake and contacted the regular Strasbourg Lodge in which I was regularized in May 1973. I informed Harry Carr who wrote to me:

I am delighted to hear that you are now within the fold [...]. Needless to say I shall be most interested to know if you have written anything suitable for us in the years when we were divorced.

However Carr retired as Secretary in November 1973. The following January, I read a paper before the lodge of research of the Grande Loge

Nationale Française, Villard de Honnecourt. It was published with proper acknowledgment for the kindness of Harry Carr and included most documents I had rediscovered.

In July 1978, I began corresponding with a PM of QC Lodge, Brigadier ACF Jackson. He suggested I enter the Norman Spencer Award Essay Competition which I did in 1986. Then he and Freddy Seal-Coon proposed my name as a full member of the Lodge.

On 11 November 2010, I became the first French Mason elected as a full member of QC. And on June 18, 2014, I demitted as I was Senior Warden of the Lodge.

3. What do you think your major contributions to Masonic research have been?

- Rediscovering in 1979 what is known nowadays as the 'Sharp Documents', a story I told as 'The Fate of some French Masonic Archives'.
- Showing in 1984 that the 'Bordeaux Constitutions of 1762' were in fact an adaptation of the 1763 Statutes of the Grand Lodge of France for Estienne Morin's Order of the Royal Secret.
- Showing that same year that the *Grande Loge Nationale Indépendante pour la France et les Colonies Françaises* (the present *Grande Loge Nationale Française*), which was recognized by UGLE on 20 November 1913, was founded by one Lodge only, which is proven by the *Histoire de la Loge Anglaise 204 de Bordeaux* written in 1913 by its Secretary, Renou.
- Showing in 2009 that Grand Commander Dalcho, in December 1821, suggested to the Cerneau representative in Charleston that Cerneau's Grand Consistory in New York and Dalcho's Supreme Council in Charleston should divide the whole territory of the United States between them.
- Showing in 2013 that the Northern Masonic Jurisdiction could not have been created lawfully in 1813.

4. What are your views about Masonic research and Masonic researchers today?

When I happen to give Masonic instruction to Apprentices or to Master Masons who wish to learn, I give them first one piece of advice: not to believe anything they are told in their lodge without asking 'How do you know ?' and not to believe either what they read in books about the history of Freemasonry without checking sources and information provided by any author. Some time ago, I wrote a paper about Masonic books – I read it once in Rome with the subtitle, the Good, the Bad and the Ugly – and quoted the following words :

If one resigns oneself to be part of a flock, a flock of Hindus, of Catholics or of Maoists, that's one thing. But if one has real breadth, and if it is one's own personal concern, one must search....

I do not use books to find answers but to find how and where their authors found out what they state.

5. What are your views about English Freemasonry both today and for the future?

I was extremely happy to discover the Address of Pro Grand Master Lord Northampton before The Cornerstone Society in 2005. I quoted parts of it in one of my books. He said for instance:

... let me stress that you cannot discover the mysteries of Freemasonry by reading the ritual book. You have to go through the process of initiation to realise and unlock the mystery, because it is a felt experience.

One year later, Bro. Julian Rees expressed a similar idea:

A peculiar system of morality, veiled in allegory and illustrated by symbols. This is the answer to the question, 'What is Freemasonry ?' [...] This is, and is intended to be, a quick answer which endeavours to describe that which, in fact, cannot be described in words of one syllable, indeed may not be described adequately in words at all.

I wish these notions were shared by most English Freemasons.

6. How does this compare with European or worldwide Freemasonry?

It could be that our approach to Freemasonry is a little different. In Europe most of us believe that initiation can modify a man (a possibility which does not always 'work'). We think that the main characteristic of Freemasonry resides in the initiations conferred by its lodges through rituals which includes symbols connected with the notion of building and that the symbol of the Great Architect of the Universe conveys them a universal dimension.

7. What are your personal plans for the future?

Keep on working!

www.ingramcontent.com/pod-product-compliance
Lightning Source LLC
Chambersburg PA
CBHW070812280326
41934CB00012B/3159